VOICES FROM CEMETERY HILL:
The Civil War Diary, Reports, and Letters of
Colonel William Henry Asbury Speer
(1861-1864)

For Doug & Jeff Jarrett –
fellow students of Southern history &
the Civil War – with warm
wishes and very best regards.

edited by
Allen Paul Speer

Allen Paul Speer
10 May 1997

The Overmountain Press
JOHNSON CITY, TENNESSEE

ISBN 1-57072-050-9

1 2 3 4 5 6 7 8 9 0

For my cousins, Frances Harding Casstevens and Lewis Shore Brumfield, whose knowledge, scholarship, love of history and devotion to Yadkin County, North Carolina, are a source of inspiration and encouragement.

Acknowledgments

I would especially like to thank all the grandchildren of Civil War veterans for the stories they shared with me. I was astonished to learn how many descendants of soldiers live in the Yadkin area and how much they remember of what their grandparents told them:

Albert Martin, my high school principal, remembers his grandfather's story of how he was with Asbury Speer at the Battle of the Wilderness. Mr. Martin's father was named for Asbury.

Fred Hobson, Sr., said his grandfather refused to talk about the war.

Dwight Matthews said his great grandmother threw hot water on an enrolling officer hiding in the woods behind a log. His great grandfather Matthews never did go to war.

Ralph Transou said the only injury his grandfather received during the war was when a pistol fell out of his grandfather's pocket and shot him through the hand. Ralph's grandfather was relieving himself at the time.

Ella Mae Mock's grandfather, along with three brothers, served in the war. She remembers the moving story of a time when her grandfather's brother was hungry, so his parents sent food in the school lunch bucket he used as a boy. Ella Mae's great uncle was deeply moved by this gesture of kindness. He died trying to defend Richmond.

Lewis Shore Brumfield said his grandfather's brother was shot for being a deserter.

Felix Harding was a young man when his grandfather died at the age of ninety. Felix remembers his grandfather told him that he was hit five times at Gettysburg.

Henry Shore said his grandfather had to eat rats to stay alive. When Henry's grandfather returned home after the war, he weighed only eighty pounds.

Thanks are also due to Masonic Lodge 162 in Yadkinville, N. C., Cleve Phillips, Helen Kinney, Margaret Eggers, Greg Mast, John Woodard, Bonnie Speer Phillips, Charles Mathis, Sam Atkinson, Ruby Bray Canipe, Paul Neal, Harvey Harding, Felix Harding, Lucy Holcomb Reece, Richard Speer, Freda Grim, Virgil Long, Felix Speer, James Speer, Richard

Jackson, Russell Taylor, Ann Speer Riley, Frieda Hinshaw Speer (my mother), and Bonnie Hinshaw (my grandmother) for all their help.

I am greatly indebted to my friends who read the manuscript and offered suggestions: Bill Watterson, Rosie Smith, Wayne Morris, Mike Joslin, John York, Jeff Minick, Fred Chappell, Fred Hobson, Jr., Mike Taylor and Todd Groce. I would also like to thank Mike Joslin for his excellent photography, Randy Hodge for drawing the battle maps, and Caren Casstevens for drawing the map of Yadkin County.

Sources used for the maps of the battles of Fredericksburg, Chancellorsville, Gettysburg, Wilderness and Spotsylvania, Spotsylvania to Petersburg, and Reams' Station are listed respectively as follows: map on page 87—Frank A. O'Reilly, *Stonewall Jackson at Fredericksburg: The Battle of Prospect Hill December 13, 1862* (Lynchburg, Virginia: H.E. Howard, Inc., 1993), p. 99; map on page 99—Ernest B. Furgurson and William J. Clipson, *Chancellorsville 1863* (New York: Vintage Books, 1993), p. 201; map on page 106—James M. McPherson, *The Atlas of the Civil War* (New York: Macmillan, Inc. 1994), p. 122; maps on pages 129 and 137—James M. McPherson, *Battle Cry of Freedom: The Civil War Era* (New York: Ballantine Books, 1988), pp. 727, 736; and map on page 148—John Horn, *The Destruction of the Weldon Railroad: Deep Bottom, Globe Tavern, and Reams' Station* (Lynchburg, Virginia: H.E. Howard, Inc., 1991), p. 160.

In addition, I would like to thank Frances Harding Casstevens for doing the typing and helping with the editing, and Lewis Shore Brumfield for his help with the research.

My main sources of encouragement came from my wife, Janet Barton Speer, and my son, Barton Carroll. Their suggestions were invaluable.

My financial support for this work was made possible by a John Stephenson fellowship awarded through the Appalachian College Association with funding provided by the Andrew Mellon Foundation. I also thank Lees-McRae College for allowing me the time and support to complete this book.

Lastly, I would like to thank my mentor for the project, Gurney Norman, and my mentor institution, the University of Kentucky.

Editor's Note

In 1980, following the death of Colonel Asbury Speer's niece Nellie Speer Dobbins, I discovered family papers dating back to the time of Aunt Nell's great great grandfather, Aaron Speer, Sr. Aaron, born in 1734, was my great great great great great grandfather. Beginning with Aaron, the papers preserved by Aunt Nell tell the compelling story of my family history. The Civil War diary and letters of Uncle Asbury Speer are only part of this rich inheritance.

Editing Asbury's papers has been a labor of love. Rarely have I seen a collection of writings so intensely personal and introspective. His words reveal a deep affection for his home and family and describe the horrible anguish he feels when he realizes he might lose them.

Asbury's first letter is written in November of 1861 and his last correspondence, mailed to Governor Zeb Vance, was dated July 29, 1864. During this span of time, Asbury's diary and letters express the full spectrum of human emotion.

Asbury Speer had an unorthodox style of writing, which was widely used during the Civil War era. His papers are filled with long, run-on sentences, sentence fragments, and, on occasion, quotation marks for punctuation. For this reason, I have added periods, capital letters, and separated some of the sentences. For the sake of readability and clarity, I have corrected Asbury's spelling and some grammar. If I was unable to identify a word, I left a blank space where the word appears in the sentence. All editorial comments are framed with brackets.

**Nellie Speer Dobbins (1886 - 1980)
This picture of Asbury's niece was
taken in 1907 at Powhatan College, Charles Town, West Virginia.**

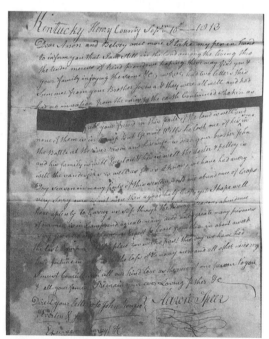

**Letter written during the War of 1812 by
Asbury's great grandfather, Aaron Speer,
Sr.**

Table of Contents

List of Photographs and Illustrations

The communication of the dead is tongued with fire
beyond the language of the living.

—T. S. Eliot

Colonel Speer's grave, near Boonville, N. C. (Photo by Mike Joslin.)

The home of Asbury's brother James can be seen from Cemetery Hill. (Photo by Mike Joslin.)

Prologue

Four months before his death and four days before the Battle of the Wilderness, Colonel William Henry Asbury Speer took pen in hand to write a poem for his family. In his verse, which turned out to be a premonition of his fate, he reflects on the meaning of suffering but accepts, without question, the existence of a transcendent being. For even though fiery battles of the Civil War consumed the lives of his friends, his faith remained firm. Asbury believed in the power of prayer. But even more, he embraced the healing power of divine love which, for him, was synonymous with home and family. It was his family's love that gave him the strength and courage to go on. Strong in his faith, he continued to fight, until finally, his pilgrimage at an end, he returned home. Asbury's father and brothers brought him back to the quiet Methodist churchyard atop Cemetery Hill.

The Dying Soldier

I am dying, comrade, dying,
Ebbs the feeble life-tide fast,
And the dark mysterious shadows,
Gather on the evening blast,

Raise heads, dear friends and listen,
To the few, faint words I speak,
Hear the last wish of a soldier,
Eno [even though] life's pulses grow too weak,

Though I came with Southern freemen,
With brave hearts and arms of might,
Gainst the foe's invading legion,
To defend our homes and right,

Though I cannot, mid the battle,
Feel my heart's exulting thrill,
Yet, I perish like a soldier,
Die a Southern patriot still,   I

Tell my noble gray-haired Father,
Here beside Potomac's wave,
That his son, his pride, his darling,
Fills a soldier's honored grave,

Tell him that the Christian's armor,
Sword of faith and shield of love,
Won my way of life eternal,
To a peaceful home above,

Tell my mother that my spirit,
Dreads not God's all-righteous frown,
That I passed to heaven triumphant,
Bore the cross and won the crown,

I am dying, comrade, dying,
Tell my heart's last filfull swell,
Tell the cold dew gathering o'er me,
Father, Mother, friends — Farewell.

> Written by me near Liberty
> Mills at camp for my Dear Father,
> Mother, Brothers and Aunt in event
> I fall in the Army May the 1st 1864.

Not far from my own father's grave (Paul Speer, Jr.), Colonel William Henry Asbury Speer, commander of the 28th Regiment North Carolina Troops during the American Civil War, is buried beside his brothers, sisters, aunt, parents, and his grandmother. The inscription on his gravestone reads, "After life's fitful fever, he sleeps well." The caption is a poignant reminder of the carnage he witnessed and the suffering he endured. Now he can rest.

It is usually spring, when cool weather lingers and the earth is an incipient green, that I visit my family on Cemetery Hill. I come to this serene resting place when the air across the valley is crystal clear and the Blue Ridge Mountains are close enough to touch. Clouded thoughts seem to disappear when the crisp breeze hits my brow, quickens my step and accompanies the sunrise music of songbirds. The chirping chorus all but overpowers creeks, hills and mountains, reminding me of verities as plain and simple as the first light of day. When dawn is breaking, I come to be with my father, to remember his life and the powerful history of this land, and to treasure forever the heroics of my uncle Asbury Speer. I will someday rest with my people in this beautiful place.

The cemetery hilltop and the valley below must look much as they did in Colonel Speer's time, although today, near the end of the twentieth century, much of the forest has been cleared to offer pastures and cornfields where cattle graze and deer are often seen. The countryside is still unspoiled, much like the landscape that existed on the eve of America's internal war of turmoil, so eloquently described by Bruce Catton:

> In 1860, most people still lived on farms or in small towns. The landscape was predominantly rural, with unending sandy roads winding leisurely across a country which was both drowsy with enjoyment of the present and vibrant with eagerness to get into the future. The average American then was in fact what he has been since only in legend, an independent, small farmer.... This may or may not have been the end of America's golden age, but it was at least the final haunted moment of its age of innocence.[1]

I realize it is naive to equate the pastoral age described by Catton with the family cemetery on my farm, but when I come to this bucolic place, sequestered from what Robert Penn Warren calls "convulsions of the world,"[2] I am at peace. I momentarily forget the madness of the twentieth century and the nervous rage that seems to animate modern life. The farm restores my sanity and is a sanctuary for my spirit.

I also find peace, and much sadness, as I read family

---

[1] Bruce Catton, The Civil War (New York: American Heritage/Bonanza Books, 1982), p. 9
[2] Robert Penn Warren, All The King's Men (New York: Harcourt Brace Jovanovich, Inc., 1974), p. 473.

papers discovered in 1980 when Nellie Speer Dobbins, a niece of Colonel Speer, passed away at the age of 94. Years earlier, she had placed the Colonel's Civil War letters, all neatly stacked and folded, inside cigar boxes, along with manuscripts written by his sisters, Annis and Nancy Jane. Their writings describe an era full of romantic sentiment, and as Catton says, the "final haunted moments of an innocent age" were passing away. As Civil War historian James McPherson observes, it "was a sentimental age when strong men were not afraid to cry (or weep as they would say), when Harriet Beecher Stowe's great novel and Stephen Foster's songs could stir genuine emotions."[3]

Discovering the family papers had a profound impact on my life. I had uncovered buried treasure from a distant past. In this world, words were oftentimes windows of the soul, symbolic tokens of affection expressing deeply felt religious beliefs. In our own time, words are not treasured nor appreciated to the same degree.

McPherson notes:

> We seldom speak or write that way anymore. Most people have not done so since WWI, which, as Ernest Hemingway and Paul Fussell have written, made such words as glory, honor, courage, hallow, sacrifice, valor, and sacred vaguely embarrassing if not mock-heroic.... But our cynicism about the genuineness of such sentiment is more our problem than theirs. It raises a barrier to our understanding of what I am convinced, after reading at least 25,000 letters and more than a hundred diaries of Civil War soldiers, were deeply felt convictions.[4]

Colonel Speer's diary and letters express a deep, abiding love of home and a heartfelt concern for his family's health and well being. In 1853 he wrote from Jonesville, North Carolina, to his sister:

> I was at Father's last week, and they were all well.

[3]James M. McPherson, What They Fought For 1861-1865, (Baton Rouge and London: Louisiana State University Press, 1994), p. 13.
[4]McPherson, pp. 12-13.

The apple trees, garden fields, and meadow all looked pleasant indeed. O! They bring back thoughts of the past when we were all enjoying the blessing of parental affections and care. These are days I dare not speak of as I am almost compelled to shed the tear of regret that I ever left my father's house.[5]

And in 1864, following a month-long furlough:

Well Father and Mother, I enjoyed my visit at home very much. It was very pleasant to me to be with you all. It is the next place to heaven to be with my Dear Father, Mother, Aunt and Brothers at home—even in times of war it is delightful and oh what it would be if peace was declared.[6]

Sentimental feelings about land and family were expressed in nearly all the letters written by Colonel Speer, his sisters and relatives, sometimes with a bit of embellishment. But there was also a dark side. Beneath the sentiment and innocence was much discontent and stress. And, to a large extent, this strife would lead to an emotional holocaust for many people. "We have rebelled against our Maker and against our government," wrote Colonel Speer's mother, and "we could not expect nothing but judgement from the Almighty.... I wish I was away from this rebel state."[7] Not only was Speer's immediate family opposed to secession, but many friends and relatives who had married or lived near Quakers for generations were also ambivalent about the war.[8] One first cousin, a Campbellite[9] preacher and abolitionist, was appointed to a diplomatic post by President Abraham Lincoln. Another first cousin, an Indiana writer and editor,

[5]W. H. A. Speer to sister, June 17, 1853 (Speer Family Papers, in private possession of Allen Paul Speer, Banner Elk, N.C.).

[6]W. H. A. Speer to father and mother, April 4, 1864 (Speer Family Papers).

[7]Elizabeth Speer to A. Jackson Ashby, August 1867 (original copy in private possession of Helen Ashby Shull, Lewistown, Ill.)

[8]Joshua Kennerly Speer III, Autobiographical Memoir, 1905 (in private possession, cited courtesy of Richard Speer, San Marcos, Cal. This work is hereafter cited as J. K. Speer Memoir).

[9]Alexander Campbell was the leader of one of the largest home grown religious movements in American history. His followers did not belong to any of the established denominations. Campbellites believed that when the Bible speaks, we speak and when the Bible is silent, we are silent. There are, today, three branches that evolved from the original movement: Disciples of Christ, Church of Christ, and the Christian Church.

believed the war was caused by "fanatical elements of the North brought in through the Republican Party."[10] This lack of agreement about the nature of the conflict, even within the immediate family, was not uncommon. Still, in spite of the strife and turmoil, it was, for the most part, an age where religious faith and romantic sentiment were greatly respected.

In his diary and letters, Colonel Speer's words express that religious sentiment, as do the words of relatives who lived and wrote and who, within the strained intimacy of one family, reflected on the meaning of suffering. Their voices speak to me with a clarity, power and conviction that, in our own time, most of us either fail to hear or do not understand.

[10]Joshua Kennerly Speer III to Dr. James Caswell Speer, no date (in private possession, cited courtesy of Virginia Metz).

Asbury Speer

Introduction

"I think of Pilot Mountain upon which I gazed with admiration when I was a boy...and the Blue Ridge...and that lovely stream—the Yadkin.... In thinking of you I am made to weep and now that I try to write I have to stop to wipe away the tears sent forth by that unfeigned love which I have for you all." (Joshua Kennerly Speer II, 1794-1858, La Vergne, Tennessee, to his niece Annis Melissa Speer, 1834-1858, Boonville, N. C., written July 1, 1856.)

These words clearly express love and affection for land and family. Colonel William Henry Asbury Speer, like his uncle Joshua and sister Annis, loved the land where his ancestors worked, lived, and died. Familiar landmarks like Pilot Mountain, the Blue Ridge, Mount Nebo and the Yadkin River graced a landscape that, when remembered, could make him weep. And it was this mystical affinity for home and the "unfeigned love" of family that we must consider when reading the diaries and letters of the Civil War era. For in Colonel Speer's papers, though he often wrote of war, he always thought of home.

Today, in homes of his descendants, the image of a bewildered man hangs on their walls. The tintype portrait reveals the startled expression of a man still perplexed by the course of events. His bearded face cannot conceal the look of puzzlement, of confusion, perhaps of fear. His eyes seem to suggest some unresolved conflict. Perhaps his expression mirrors the complexities of the age or the contradictions of his nature, or possibly the horror of watching the inexorable weight of war crush what he most loved—his home and family.

The photograph of Asbury Speer is, in fact, an accurate depiction of an enigmatic man. He opposed secession but was proud to be a Southern patriot. He was ambivalent about staying in the army, even though he served as Colonel of the Yadkin militia for over a decade.

In March of 1863, he wrote, "I have looked at it on all sides, and have my mind fully made up to leave the service as

Joshua Kennerly Speer II (1794-1858)
Asbury's uncle Joshua, Aquilla's brother, was an original
trustee of Jonesville Methodist Academy in 1818. Joshua
later became a Campbellite minister in Tennessee. His
daughter, America, married Asbury's brother Aaron. Joshua
was also the father of Dr. E.A. Speer and William Sheppard
Speer. (Photo used by permission of Richard Speer, a great
great grandson of Joshua.)

Asbury Speer as Colonel in the Yadkin militia.

soon as I can."[1]

In addition, Asbury debated whether giving his life for Southern independence was worth his last full measure of devotion. In poor health, he weighed his options: "...in trying to do my duty, I do not think that I ought to endanger my health, for self-preservation is the first law of nature. I know my health is in a delicate condition and I have been feeling our Dr. as to a certificate of disability to resign upon ..."[2]

Finding the delicate balance between duty and ambition was difficult for Asbury. "I know that I am a little ambitious," wrote Speer, "but not to heap upon myself worldly honors further than to do my duty as a man and anything short of that I would think dishonorable to myself.... I had rather be a good man and wise than to be in the place of General Lee."[3] His obvious ambivalence about the meaning of honor is a theme in his diary and letters. On more than one occasion he chastised deserters for shirking their responsibilities, yet he did not hesitate to use every legal device at his disposal to keep his younger brother James from being drafted. He wrote: "I got a new lot of papers for James...so that there is no danger of their doing anything with him. General Lane is gone on furlough and I got Col. Barbour, who is in command of the Brigade, to approve the papers officially...."[4]

To better understand Asbury's character, one must reach back into his past. This complex individual's background may have contributed to the ambiguities that would later cause his internal debates.

Colonel Speer's ancestors were Ulster Scots from Northern Ireland who, during the last half of the seventeenth century, settled on the eastern shore of Maryland. Nearly one hundred years before the Speers moved to the Yadkin Valley (the Huntsville-Shallowford area), they mingled with, and later married, their peace-loving Quaker neighbors. Relatives like the Kennerlys and Everndons (English) were revered and

---

[1]Asbury Speer to father, March 13, 1863 (Speer Family Papers).
[2]ibid.
[3]ibid.
[4]ibid.

James M. Speer (1843-1928)
Asbury's brother James was the father of Nellie Speer and Aaron S.
Speer. Aaron was my great grandfather and James was my great great
grandfather.

their surnames used by members of the Speer family for generations. From the 1680s until 1861, Asbury's ancestors lived in or near Quaker settlements. For Asbury not to be affected by Quaker pacifism would be highly unusual, especially since his first cousin Aquilla Spencer Speer was a devout member of the Society of Friends.[5]

Not only was religion a factor that contributed to Asbury's confusion, but, also, the level of education his family received unquestionably influenced his indecisiveness. He came from a diverse, well-educated family.

Speer's brothers and sisters attended Jonesville Methodist Academy. His intellectual sisters, Annis Melissa and Nancy Jane, went on to graduate from Greensboro Female College. Nancy Jane Speer pursued further studies at Mount Holyoke before becoming Principal of Rockford Female Seminary. Speer's brother Aaron graduated from Union Institute (later to become Trinity College and then Duke University) and, during the 1850-51 school year, was appointed Professor of English Literature and Natural Science.[6] Asbury's brother "Vet" (S. T. Speer), a student at Jonesville Academy in 1850, was later Sheriff of Yadkin County during the Civil War. In 1863 and 1864, Sheriff Speer's life was in danger as the antiwar movement in Yadkin became more volatile.

The decade preceding the move to Southern independence was eventful for Asbury Speer. As early as 1850, Asbury was a Colonel in the Yadkin County militia and superintendent of a tannery in Jonesville, North Carolina.[7] He prospered in Jonesville, where he lived for at least twelve years. His political future looked bright. In 1856 and 1858, he represented Yadkin County in the North Carolina House of Commons. He lost the 1860 State Senate race to Joseph Dobson, even though he carried the county. In 1861, with war imminent, his political career was temporarily halted. Although now,

---

[5]The history of the Speer family in Maryland has been well documented by the following genealogists: Virgil Long, Seymour, Indiana; Freda Grim, Baltimore, Maryland ; Richard Speer, San Marcos, Cal.; Kathleen Much, Menlo Park, Cal.

[6]Nora C. Chaffin, Trinity College 1839-1892: The Beginnings of Duke University (Durham: Duke University Press, 1950), pp. 134, 136.

[7]Ruby Bray Canipe, Early Elkin-Jonesville History and Genealogy (Jonesville, N. C.: Tarheel Graphics, 1981), p. 88.

with secession at hand and with years of militia experience under his belt, opportunities for advancement in the Confederate army seemed to be quite promising. He was aware of the fact that political success often follows the heroes of war. Even so, Asbury was ambivalent about military advancement.

His reticence might be attributed to his ethics. In 1853, he wrote to his sister, "Everything is for the better to them that do right."[8] Yet his honor was tested, not only by war but by relationships with "Dixie ladies." A bit more information about his past may help us better understand the nature of certain alleged improprieties.

According to Asbury's service record from the National Archives in Washington, D. C., he had light colored hair, florid skin and was 5 feet 10 inches tall. His high forehead, full beard, piercing gaze and deep-set eyes reveal a handsome, yet inscrutable countenance.

Asbury was fond of the ladies. In 1862, when he was a prisoner of war at Governor's Island, N. Y., he wrote in his diary: "The N. Y. ladies have come over to see the Secessionists. If they were only Dixie ladies, how I would...like to gaze upon them. O! they cannot love like our Southern ladies nor make half such loving companions."

Asbury was sentimental, compassionate and loyal to his family, but, as mentioned, circumstantial evidence suggests he was somewhat cavalier in his relationships with women. On March 15, 1850, he married Miss Kitty Chamberlain, a union that is something of a family mystery. In an autobiography written by his first cousin Joshua Kennerly Speer III, it was noted that Asbury never married. Asbury's nieces and nephews claimed he was a bachelor. Yet, the March 28, 1850, Salisbury *Daily Watchman* states, "Married in Surry County, on the 15th inst., by the Rev. Tho. Hains, Col. W. H. A. Speer, and Miss Kitty Chamberlain." Though no records, documents or graves have been found to shed light on Miss Kitty's fate, there was, however, a paternity suit filed against Colonel

[8]W. H. A. Speer to sister June 17, 1853 (Speer Family Papers).

Asbury's sister Nancy Jane Speer (1828-1857) attended Jonesville Methodist Academy and graduated from Greensboro Female College. She pursued further studies at Mount Holyoke before becoming principal of Rockford Female Seminary.

Asbury's brother S. T. "Vet" Speer (1837-1890) was Civil War Sheriff of Yadkin County (1862-1866), Clerk of Superior Court (1867-1868), and County Commissioner (1870-1872). (Photo used by permission of Ann Speer Riley, a great granddaughter of Vet Speer.)

Asbury's brother Aaron Clinton Speer (1831-1856) was appointed Professor of Literature and Natural Science at Union Institute (later to become Trinity College) in 1851. He spent the next three years in Tennessee and, for a time, was editor of the *Tennessee Patriot*. During his stay there, he joined the Christian Church and married his first cousin America H. Speer, a daughter of Joshua Kennerly Speer II. In February of 1854, he moved to Boonville, Missouri, where he published the *Boonville Missourian*. In 1855, he opened a school in Independence, Missouri. On the 6th of September 1855, he returned to the family farm in North Carolina, hoping to recover from consumption. He died February 1, 1856, and was buried in the Methodist churchyard on Cemetery Hill.

Speer two years after the marriage. It reads as follows:

State of North Carolina, April the 17th, 1852
Yadkin County.

Examination of Elizabeth Bully before me Thos Haynes a justice of the peace in and for said county in case of bastardy she states on oath that, the child which she is Big with does belong to W. H. A. Spear [Speer] that said Spare [Speer] came to her hose [house] several times and that he had connection with her more than one hundred times [but] that she don't know where nor when the child was got. She thinks Spare [Speer] is the father of the child from the way he don[e] it. he don[e] it better than any body else, tho [though there was no] man but Spare [Speer], were [where] one more man ever had anything to do with me and that has been two years ago this April the 17th 1852.

Thos. Haynes JP   X
                    [Elizabeth Bulley's mark][9]

One clue to a better understanding of Speer's character is in an 1856 letter from his uncle, the Campbellite Joshua Kennerly Speer II: "O that cousin Asbury, Do exhort him every time you see him to be a Christian." Asbury, as we know from a letter,[10] did not join the church until the spring of 1863.

Another clue surfaced in 1960. An elderly lady, claiming to be Asbury's illegitimate daughter, came to the family farm. She said her father was unable to have children, so he selected Asbury as the surrogate father. According to her, Speer honored her father's request. Asbury was home for a month-long furlough in the spring of 1864, which might lend credibility to her claim.

Certainly, Asbury's integrity was tested by romantic rela-

[9]Bastardy Bond Files of Yadkin County, North Carolina, Division of Archives and History, Raleigh, N. C., abstracts from loose papers compiled by Lewis Shore Brumfield.
[10]W. H. A. Speer to father & mother, April 28, 1863 (Speer Family Papers).

Elizabeth Forbes, wife of British General John Forbes, is buried behind Asbury's grandfather, Aaron Speer, Jr. Most of the graves in the old cemetery are unmarked. Elizabeth Forbes is my sixth great grandmother. (Photo by Mike Joslin.)

tionships, but we can only guess whether marital infidelity occurred in the case of Elizabeth Bulley. Miss Kitty Chamberlain could have easily died having her first child, or Bulley might have falsely accused an innocent man. There is simply not enough information available to form conclusions.

However, we can be more certain about Asbury's character on the field of battle, as his diary and letters reveal. The arduous service demanded of him deepened his commitment to the Southern cause. For in spite of poor health, opposition to secession, ambivalence about religious beliefs, misgivings about military service, and concern for his younger brother James, he did his duty. From the beginning of the conflict, he was determined to defend his home.

In April of 1861, when Lincoln called for volunteers to suppress the rebellion in the lower South, Asbury, like many

Yadkinians, became a staunch defender of Southern rights. He strongly opposed Lincoln's attempts to coerce a recalcitrant South. He chose to fight.

During the war, Asbury would lead his company and, later, his regiment in numerous battles, miraculously surviving them all until on August 25, 1864, three months into the siege of Petersburg, he fell mortally wounded at the Battle of Reams' Station. Struck in the head by a piece of shell that, as his mother said, "broke his skull," he died four days later in a Petersburg hospital.[11] His body was then loaded into a wagon and brought back to Providence Methodist Church near Boonville, North Carolina, for burial. The church, located on land where Colonel Speer spent his childhood, burned in 1870, but the cemetery has been used by his family ever since.

Asbury Speer's long journey home reminds me of the final words of Stonewall Jackson, "Let us cross over the river and rest under the shade of the trees." Colonel Speer crossed the Yadkin River for the last time in September of 1864 and was buried on land farmed by his ancestors for nearly one hundred years. He was laid to rest close to his grandmother, Elizabeth Forbes Jones Speer, a granddaughter of British General John Forbes. Asbury had often heard his grandmother's stories about his great great grandfather. General Forbes, who named Pittsburgh and opened a major road of western expansion, was Colonel George Washington's commanding officer in the French and Indian War. Forbes died on March 11, 1759, at the age of forty-nine.[12] His wife, Elizabeth, lived the final years of her life with her daughter, Elizabeth Forbes Jones, and was buried in an older Speer cemetery that lies untended in an open field just across the valley from where her granddaughter and Asbury rest. Most of the graves there are unmarked, and the marked graves are barely discernable. Elizabeth's stone only bears a faint "E F." The rest

---

[11]Elizabeth Speer to A. Jackson Ashby, August, 1867 (original copy in private possession of Helen Ashby Shull).

[12]"Forbes, John," in The Encyclopedia Americana International Edition (Danbury, Connecticut: Grolier, Inc., 1989), p. 55. Hugh Rankin, "John Forbes," Encyclopedia of World Biography (New York: McGraw-Hill, 1973).

Aquilla Speer (1804-1888)
A leader in the Methodist church for over fifty years, Asbury's father, Aquilla, was also a justice of the peace as early as 1834. After the war, he served three terms as county commissioner. The inscription on his gravestone reads, "He was a friend to the poor." Aquilla is my great great great grandfather.

has vanished. In the letters and memoirs written by Asbury's father and cousins, General Forbes is often mentioned.[13]

Besides Forbes, two of the strongest influences on Asbury Speer were his grandfather Aaron Speer, Jr., and Aaron's first cousin Henry Speer. According to one account, Aaron Speer, Jr., was "the most noted member of the family of his time as a teacher and a man of learning. He farmed, taught school, and was a clerk of the Superior Court of what was then known as Surry County."[14]

Aaron Jr.'s first cousin Henry Speer was another prominent official in colonial Surry (Yadkin). Henry's name appears in early court records more often than any other political figure. A captain in the American Revolution, Henry would later "survey nearly all of Surry and Yadkin county." After the close of the Revolutionary War, he was a legislator in the General Assembly in Raleigh, county commissioner, land speculator, road overseer, justice-of-the-peace, town commissioner of Rockford, commissioner for the formation of Wilkes County, and, in 1787, builder of a bridge over South Deep Creek near Shallowford. While the original bridge is not standing, the road that crosses a modern bridge still bears his name. Even with advancing age, Henry was not to sit back idle; but sometime after 1800, he accepted the challenge of Kentucky and the new Northwestern territories beyond the Appalachians. Where, when, or how he died is a mystery still. Henry's record of accomplishment set a standard that Speer descendants were hard pressed to follow.[15]

Forbes, Henry, and Aaron, Jr., passed on a family tradition that undoubtedly affected Asbury's choice of politics and the

[13]Aquilla Speer to William Sheppard Speer (no date). It is believed that Aquilla wrote this letter to his nephew in 1880 (in private possession, cited courtesy of Richard Speer, a great grandson of William Sheppard Speer. Also, in autobiographical memoirs written by Sheppard Speer in 1893 and by Joshua Kennerly Speer III in 1905, Forbes's influence is noted.

[14]J. K. Speer Memoir. In Surry Court Minutes, Aaron Speer, Jr., is listed as constable and coroner, but I can find no record that he served as Clerk of Court.

[15]Frances Harding Casstevens, "Samuel Speer, Surveyor," in Heritage of Yadkin County, North Carolina, ed. Frances Harding Casstevens (Winston-Salem, N. C.: Hunter Publishing Company, 1981), p. 616; Johnson J. Hayes, The Land of Wilkes (Wilkesboro, N. C.: Wilkes County Historical Society, 1962), p. 33; Fred Hughes, "Historic Land Grant Map of Yadkin County," (Jamestown, N. C.: The Custom House, 1978). Also, on Oct. 9, 1852, in Fayette County, Kentucky, Peter Eddleman, age 90, stated in his pension application that he enlisted in 1780 (age 18) under Captain Speer in Surry County. Eddleman wrote, "I moved to Kentucky near where I now live in 1793. Captain Speer used to call here on his way through the country. He moved to Indiana many years since and I have heard and believe...that he died there."

military as professions. However, Asbury's father, Aquilla, was a pacifist, which confused Asbury even more. Aquilla Speer was "a leader in the Methodist Church, and among the first temperance lecturers in the county, having organized the Providence Temperance Society in the forties [1840s]."[16] A deeply religious man, Aquilla opposed war; but like his father, Aaron, Jr., he was active in politics. According to court minutes recorded February 11, 1834, "Agreeable to a commission from the Governor...Aquilla Speer qualified as a justice of the peace."[17] In 1868, he served the first of his three terms as county commissioner. This achievement would have been difficult, if not impossible, had Aquilla been a secessionist.

After the war, Yadkin County quickly turned Republican and has remained, to this day, one of the strongest Republican counties in the state. The ongoing loyalty to the Republican Party shows how much hatred was spawned by secession. This was certainly true for Asbury's family. As one can tell from the tone of his letters, Speer's parents opposed secession and wanted him out of the army. Not only were they Methodists,[18] pacifists, and Unionists but, most importantly, the family was devastated by numerous tragedies. Aquilla and his wife Elizabeth had already lost four children to consumption, three dying in their twenties. The thought of losing Asbury was unbearable. But they had to deal with the possible consequences when he went to war in 1861. The only son remaining at home was James (my great great grandfather) who they feared would have to join the Confederate army at any time.

Colonel Asbury Speer was determined to protect his younger brother James from the Conscription Act of 1862. Until the time of his death, he looked for ways to keep his brother from being drafted. On April 4, 1864, four months

---

[16]J. K. Speer Memoir.

[17]Wanda Carter Craaybeek, "Abstracts from Surry County Court Minutes, Pleas and Quarterly Sessions," on microfilm at Surry Community College Library, Dobson, N. C.

[18]There were many Methodists in Yadkin who opposed the war. In interviews with Dwight Matthews, who had two grandfathers in the war; Albert Martin, whose grandfather fought with Asbury at Wilderness; and Fred Hobson, Sr., grandson of Civil War Veteran John Hobson, it was pointed out to me that several Methodist churches in the county split because of the conflict.

before his death, Speer wrote, "I spoke to Governor Vance about constables, magistrates and militia...he told me he should not give them up but was going to keep them at home, which will save James and I am glad of it."[19] James never went to war.

It was, in fact, the problem of divided loyalties that plagued all families in Yadkin County before, during, and after the war. As mentioned in the Prologue, many of Speer's friends and relatives were Quakers. Many, but not all, of these Yadkin Quakers were against war, slavery and secession. Equally important were the Whig Unionists[20] in Yadkin who also opposed secession. When Colonel Speer, a Whig Unionist, ran against Crawford Wade Williams, a Democrat, in the 1856 election for the North Carolina House of Commons, the Whigs in Yadkin won the election by a comfortable margin—this in a political race where eleven of fourteen western counties supported Democratic gubernatorial candidate Thomas Bragg.[21] In subsequent Yadkin elections, similar voting patterns prevailed. In fact, Whigs carried the county in 1856, 1858 and 1860.[22] Precinct voting returns for these elections are listed in Appendix I.

As the numbers indicate, as late as 1860 Yadkin was a bastion of Whig strength. In addition, the county had a smaller slave population than eleven western North Carolina counties.[23] Still, there are other factors to consider. Yadkin did have large plantations, like the estate owned by Speer's cousin, Tyre Glenn. Yet even Glenn, the largest landowner and slaveholder in the county, strongly opposed secession. Other prominent figures like North Carolina Chief Justice Richmond Pearson, congressman Richard C. Puryear, and gentleman planter Nicholas Williams, who managed to

---

[19]W. H. A. Speer to father and mother, April 4, 1864 (Speer Family Papers).

[20]Whigs believed secession was unconstitutional. They wanted the federal government to promote economic growth, build roads, and provide the internal improvements that the back country desperately needed. They could not see how Southern independence would help their cause.

[21]John C. Inscoe, Mountain Masters, Slavery, and the Sectional Crisis in Western North Carolina (Knoxville: University of Tennessee Press, 1989), p. 169.

[22]Yadkin County Record of Elections (1856-1861), North Carolina Division of Archives and History, Raleigh.

[23]Inscoe, p. 63.

Richmond Mumford Pearson (1805-1878)
Chief Justice of N. C. Supreme Court (1858-1878)
As Chief Justice, Pearson was a thorn in the side of the Confederacy. Having little sympathy for the Confederate cause, he repeatedly held the Conscription Act to be unconstitutional. When conscripts appealed their cases to Judge Pearson, as did Asbury's brother James, Pearson turned them loose. (Photo used by permission of the Department of Cultural Resources, N. C. Division of Archives and History.)

keep all three of his sons out of the war, were constitutional Unionists.[24] Also, in the February 1861 election to decide whether a convention should be held to consider secession, 1,490 Yadkinians voted against having the convention while only 34 supported the proposal.[25] "Contrary to what most historians have concluded," writes William C. Harris, "the area of greatest Union strength was the central and upper Piedmont, not the mountain counties."[26] Joseph Sitterson and Daniel Crofts agree. Crofts says that "Confederates never effectively controlled parts of the Quaker belt in Piedmont, North Carolina."[27] Consequently, as one might suspect, when fighting commenced, there were many who "hid out, refused to serve or deserted."[28] And there were those like Colonel Speer who opposed secession but still fought to the bitter end. "I cannot lay out in the woods to keep out of the way of enrolling officers," wrote Speer, responding to a letter from his parents. "And I am determined, if I live, to tell the people what I think of secession and those who advocate it."[29]

According to historian James McPherson, "Negative sentiments [about the war] seem to have been stronger among soldiers from North Carolina than any other state. This may help to explain why the desertion rate was highest in North Carolina regiments."[30]

The desertion problem was often mentioned in Speer's letters, but comments about deserters undermining the cause did not deter him from trying to prevent his brother James from being drafted, nor did it make it easier for him to resolve his ambivalence about fighting for Southern independence. "I do not wonder at secessionists being alarmed," he wrote,

---

[24]Lewis Shore Brumfield, Chief Justice Pearson and His Students (Yadkinville, N. C.: by the author, 1993), p. 18.
[25]Yadkin County Record of Elections (1861), North Carolina Division of Archives and History, Raleigh, N. C.
[26]William C. Harris, North Carolina and the Coming of the Civil War (Raleigh, N. C.: Division of Archives and History, 1988), p. 45.
[27]Daniel W. Crofts, Reluctant Confederates (Chapel Hill, N. C. and London: The University of North Carolina Press, 1989), p. 347; Joseph Carlyle Sitterson, The Secession Movement in North Carolina (Chapel Hill, N. C.: The University of North Carolina Press, 1939), p. 218.
[28]Lewis Shore Brumfield, Timothy Williams Folks (Yadkinville, N. C.: by the author, 1990), p. 47.
[29]W. H. A. Speer to father, February 18, 1864 (Speer Family Papers).
[30]James M. McPherson, What They Fought For 1861-1865 (Baton Rouge and London: Louisiana State University Press, 1994), p. 16.

State of North Carolina,
Yadkin County

This Certifies that an election opened and held at the several precincts in Yadkin County, on the 28th day of February, 1861, for State Convention to take into consideration federal relations, there were thirty-four votes polled for the Convention, and fourteen hundred and ninety votes polled against the Convention.

Sworn to and subscribed before me at office in Yadkinville the first day of March 1861.

Tehautia g. A. Joyce &c

A true copy

Convention Vote
(Used by permission of Dept. of Cultural Resources, N. C. Division of Archives and History, Raleigh.)

"they are the 'cause' of the war. I do not believe God had any-more hand in bringing the war than the 'child unborn did.'"[31]

If Speer's support for secession was, at best, lukewarm, then his neighbors back home were even more opposed to the war effort, especially after the Conscription Act passed the Confederate Congress in April of 1862. Like Chief Justice Pearson, who believed the act to be unconstitutional, many Yadkin residents refused to acknowledge that the rebel government in Richmond could legally force them to serve in the Confederate army.

If the county had been split between secessionists and anti-secessionists after Lincoln's call for troops on April 15, 1861, then momentum definitely shifted to the antiwar side when conscription started. According to John Barrett, "In early 1863, conscription reached a critical stage when twenty to thirty conscripts lodged themselves in a Yadkin County school house and fought a pitched battle with a small squad of militia, each side suffering a few casualties. Following this little affair, the situation in the mountains got practically beyond the control of the military."[32]

"This little affair," as Barrett says, came to be known as the shootout at the Quaker school house (or the Bond School house). The Bond School house fight, more than any other single event, illustrates how the war in Yadkin became "one big family squabble." For many families, "this little affair" was a malignancy that festered until it made them sick with grief and, finally, mute with rage. Generations would pass before those affected could speak openly about the Bond School, or the war, or the oppressive sadness that paralyzed their families. Even part of the Crawford Wade Williams clan, who before secession were Democrats, became Quakers and strong Republicans. "After the Civil War, five Quaker churches were started in Williams' territory—Pilot View, Union Cross, Mt. Carmel, Forbush, and East Bend—where there had been no churches before."[33]

---

[31]W. H. A. Speer to father, February 18, 1864 (Speer Family Papers).
[32]John G. Barrett, The Civil War in North Carolina (Chapel Hill, N. C.: University of North Carolina Press, 1963), p. 35.
[33]Brumfield, pp. 49, 50.

The War

"Forced marches, short rations, often no rations at all for days together, marching over roads knee deep in mud, wading rivers to the arm pits, lying in line of battle in snow, rain and hail—add to this the sudden death of best friends - brothers fallen by your side in the strife of deadly conflict - and then a faint idea is only given of the hardships, privations, bereavements and services, suffered and rendered by this veteran Regiment." (Colonel Samuel D. Lowe, Roll of Honor, 28th Regiment, N. C. Troops, N. C. State Archives, Raleigh)

Asbury Speer enlisted in the Confederate army on August 13, 1861, along with friends and cousins from Yadkin County. He was elected Captain in Company I of the 28th Regiment of North Carolina Troops.[34] When, in September of 1861, his company crossed the Yadkin River and entered Salem, North Carolina, his troops were enthusiastically received by the hometown crowds. The excitement of the Salem citizens was reported in the town's newspaper, the *People's Press*. The article reads as follows:

On Friday evening of last week the "Yadkin Stars," a Volunteer company from Yadkin County, under the command of Capt. Speer, were met a short distance beyond Winston, by a number of our citizens, the Dixie Boys, and the Salem Brass Band, when R. L. Patterson, Esq., addressed the company in his usual felicitous manner; after which they were escorted to our hotels, where they were entertained until Saturday morning, when, after a return of thanks by Capt. Speer, in behalf of his men, to the citizens of Salem for the hospitality extended to them, they departed for their temporary destination,—High Point.

This is a fine company of able bodied men, numbering ninety-odd, we believe. And we were pleased to

---

[34]The sources for the history of the 28th Regiment of North Carolina Troops are given in Louis H. Manarin and W. T. Jordan, Jr., eds. North Carolina Troops 1861-1865 (Raleigh, N. C.: North Carolina Division of Archives and History, 1866-93), Vol. XIII, pp. 99-100, hereafter cited as *N. C. Troops*; Walter Clark, ed., Histories of the Several Regiments and Battalions from North Carolina in the Great War 1861-1865, 5 vols. (Raleigh, N. C.: E. M. Uzzell, 1901, Vol 2, pp. 467-484, hereafter cited as N. C. Regiments.

see Hon. R. C. Puryear and other prominent men among the citezens [sic] of Yadkin, accompanying the "Stars" to this place, which affords another striking evidence, in connection with the enthusiasm which prevailed, of the unaminity of feeling which pervades all classes in regard to the great crisis in which is involved the weal or woe of the Southern Confederacy.[35]

On September 30, 1861, the regiment left Camp Fisher near High Point and was transported to Wilmington, North Carolina. When the Union army attacked New Bern in the spring of 1862, the 28th was ordered to the town's defense, but arriving late, they had to retreat to Kinston. At Kinston, the regiment became part of General Branch's brigade. Following Branch's death at the Battle of Antietam, James Henry Lane, Colonel of the 28th, was promoted to Brigadier General and, until the surrender at Appomattox, did a masterful job commanding the brigade. The history of the 28th Regiment is also the history of the Branch-Lane brigade, which served under Robert E. Lee's command in the Army of Northern Virginia.

It was in Virginia, at Hanover Court House, that the 28th Regiment fought its first major battle. On May 26, 1862, the rebels spent a miserable night in the mud and rain. The next morning the regiment was overrun by the Vth U. S. Army Corps under the command of General Fitz John Porter. In his diary, Asbury wrote:

> The enemy was in sixty yards of us when fire commenced.... I seen a shell strike a young Mr. Roberts of Co. A (Surry County) injuring him badly [and] fracturing both his thighs, from which he died. I also seen two more men of Co. A killed with shells, taking off the top of one of their heads and cutting the other in two.

In this battle, Asbury's company was backed up against a river. Speer writes in his diary that he could have escaped

---

[35]Salem, N. C. People's Press 20 Sept. 1861, p. 1.

Lawrence O'Bryan Branch
Appointed Colonel 33rd Regiment N.C.T. September 20, 1861.
Appointed Brigadier General on January 17, 1862. General Branch
was mortally wounded at the Battle of Antietam. (Photo from Clark,
N. C. Regiments, 1901.)

James Henry Lane
Served as Colonel of the 28th Regiment N.C.T. Served as Brigadier
General in command of the brigade tht included the 7th, 37th, 33rd,
18th, and 28th Regiments, N.C.T. (Photo from Clark, N. C. Regiments,
1901.)

by swimming the river, but his men, who could not swim, begged him to stay. They were all taken prisoner.

The prisoners were first sent to Fort Columbus, on Governor's Island in New York harbor, where they were treated very well. After a short period of time, some of the prisoners, Asbury included, were transferred to Johnson's Island on Lake Erie. According to Asbury, the prison there was "a square lot of 16⅔ acres of land enclosed with a heavy slab of plank fence 15 feet high and very strongly made. The top of the fence was filled with spike nails, so you could not press the weight of your hands on them." Asbury was soon horrified to hear tales of sentinels firing into prisoners' rooms. On August 8, 1862, Speer wrote in his diary:

> This evening, about 9½ o'clock P.M., there was one of our officers shot dead at his own quarters, just as he was going to bed. It was a cold, willful and premeditated murder.... He was a young man, a very peaceable, quiet fellow.

Not long after this incident, Asbury left Johnson's Island in a prisoner exchange. According to his service record, he was sent to Vicksburg on September 1, 1862, promoted to Major on November 1, and by December 1862 was back in Virginia. He was later promoted to Lieutenant Colonel on March 12, 1863, and Colonel on July 9, 1864.

The spring of 1863 was difficult for the 28th Regiment. On April 6, 1863, Speer wrote to his parents:

> The snow is four inches deep.... It is very cold. We have [had] much bad weather this spring — snow, rain, mud. We don't have more than two or three clear days at a time. As soon as the weather clears off & the roads get dry the army will commence moving...for neither army can move much without a fight, for there is nothing between us but the River.

And fight they did. Chancellorsville turned out to be one of the bloodiest battles of the war.

Lee, with 60,000 men, held the Rappahannock line (this is the river Speer mentioned); and Hooker, the commander of the Union army, tried to attack the Confederate flank. The movement began on April 27, 1863, and seemed about to succeed, but Hooker hesitated and, on April 30, withdrew his troops to a defensive position at Chancellorsville. The next day Lee left a small force at Fredericksburg and moved to attack Hooker. He sent Stonewall Jackson to attack Hooker's right while he struck in front. The attack on May 2 cut the Northern army in two. In a letter written May 7, 1863, Asbury described the horror of battle:

> There was a Yankee hospital caught on fire & burnt up some 500 of their wounded.... The woods caught fire from shells & burnt up hundreds of their dead and wounded, [and] some of ours...too bad to think of.... I want to see you all very badly. I would nearly give my life for the privilege. I hope you have a fine spring. The trees are just putting out here. Tell Jimmy to plant plenty of potatoes & raise some sugar cane for molasses.

Chancellorsville was a Southern victory, but a terrible price was paid—Stonewall Jackson was shot by his own men. Unfortunately, someone from Lane's Brigade was responsible for the shooting. In his diary Asbury wrote:

> I was under heavy shelling last night.... In making the first charge, we shot several of our own men— Genls. Jackson & Hill & one of Genl. Hill's aids; [they were] wounded about midnight.[36]

Jackson lost his left arm, and died several days later from pneumonia. General Lee said he lost his ablest general and "right arm" when he lost Stonewall Jackson.

With the momentum of a Southern victory at Chancellorsville, Lee decided to move north. One month later he was engaged in the greatest battle ever fought in the western hemisphere, the battle of Gettysburg.

On July 2, 1863, the day before the Pickett-Pettigrew charge assaulted the heights of Cemetery Hill, Speer wrote

---

[36]Lil Thompson, "The Sun 'Hid His Face,'" Winston-Salem Journal and Sentinel, May 6, 1962, Section C, p. 1. Hereafter cited as Lil Thompson article. (Asbury kept two diaries during the war. The only written account of the second diary that I have been able to find appeared in this 1962 Thompson article. I am still trying to track down the second diary or, at least, photocopies of that diary.)

in his diary:

> The roar of artillery and small arms was such as
> mortal man never heard before. It has been a cloudy
> day, as if the sun had hid his face from the sight of
> slaughter and bloodshed.

And on July 3:

> We charged the batteries 1½ miles over a plain. O
> such slaughter never was seen. We lost ⅔ of our Regt.
> O my God, where will this slaughter end?[37]

Colonel Samuel Lowe, who commanded the 28th Regiment
at the time of Pickett's charge, also noted that two-thirds of
the regiment was killed, wounded or missing. According to
General James Henry Lane:

> Colonel Lowe was wounded [in the charge] and
> had to leave, but Lieutenant Colonel Speer speaks
> in high terms of the bravery of his officers and men
> during the whole of that desperate and hard fought
> battle.[38]

For Colonel Lowe, the wound may have been a blessing in
disguise, because some of the bloodiest battles of the war
were yet to be fought.

After Gettysburg, Lowe was unable to sustain the energy
necessary for fighting and marching; and as a result of this
disability, Lieutenant Colonel Speer was forced to assume
command of the regiment.[39] With Speer leading the 28th, and
with Lane's Brigade covering Lee's retreat from Pennsylvania,
the Confederate army limped back to its lair in Virginia to
nurse its wounds. Yet, at Gettysburg, the gallantry of the
28th Regiment was noticed. According to historian James I.
Robertson, Jr., the Branch-Lane Brigade "would achieve a
record for valor equaled by few units North or South."[40]

The Battle of Gettysburg was the turning point of the war;
and with the Confederate defeat, momentum shifted to the

---

[37]Lil Thompson article.
[38]The United States War Department. The War of the Rebellion: A Compilation of the Official Records of the Union and Confederate Armies. 70 vols. in 128 parts (Washington, D.C.: Government Printing Office, 1880-1901), Series 1, Vol. 27, pt. 2, pp. 289-688, hereafter cited as OR.
[39]OR, Series 1, Vol. 42, pt. 2, pp. 159, 1268.
[40]James I. Robertson, Jr, General A. P. Hill (New York: Vintage Books, 1987), p. 60.

Samuel Lowe
Colonel, 28th Regiment N.C.T. wounded at Gettysburg on July 3, 1863. (Photo from Clark, N. C. Regiments, 1901.)

Army of the Potomac. By the spring of 1864, a bloody war of attrition had begun. From early May until the second week in June, Federal General U. S. Grant would lose nearly as many men as were under Lee's entire command. No matter how many men Grant lost, he had more to replace them. Robertson notes that beginning with the Battle of the Wilderness, a fight commenced that "...would last until the end of the war, with the two armies locked in almost daily combat until Appomattox mercifully brought it all to an end."[41]

A month after the Battle of the Wilderness, Speer wrote to his parents: "I am almost give out—this is 32 days we have been fighting and I have been under fire every day.... Oh Father and Mother I want to live to see you all again. Certainly this war will soon close—such slaughter can't be stood long. Pray for me."[42] Shortly after this letter was written, the siege of Petersburg began. "It is very strange to me that our genls [generals] will keep charging breastworks," wrote Speer. The breastworks (fortified trenches) around Petersburg became a maze of entrenchments and wooden obstructions. "The works we are now in," continued Speer, "are so close to the enemy's line we can't stick up our heads without getting shot at.... I tell you dear Father it is horrible to be in this place. We are first shot down—day or night—any time.... As soon as a man shows his head he is plugged [shot] at & often killed or wounded. It is a perfect state of horror here."[43]

On July 29th, Speer wrote Governor Zeb Vance after "a hard days fight in which I have lost nearly 100 men."[44] He informed Vance of the voting in the 28th Regiment (Vance 179, Holden 31). In this election, Vance was reelected Governor and Speer was elected to the North Carolina Senate. Asbury never served his term in office. One month later he was dead. Weeks before his death, he offered his final words to his family. "I am almost crazy," he wrote. "The weather is awful hot & dry—no rain since the 12th of May—everything

---

[41]Robertson, p. 253.
[42]Asbury Speer to father, mother, aunt and brothers, June 5, 1864 (Speer Family Papers).
[43]W. H A. Speer to father and mother, June 25, 1864 (Speer Family Papers).
[44]Colonel W. H. A. Speer to Governor Zebulon Vance, July 29, 1864 (Vance Papers, North Carolina Division of Archives and History, Raleigh, North Carolina).

Zebulon Baird Vance was the Civil War Governor of North Carolina. Before he was elected governor in 1862, he served as Colonel of the 26th Regiment N.C.T. (Photo used by permission of Dept. of Cultural Resources, N. C. Division of Archives and History, Raleigh.)

is nearly burnt up.... It looks like the enemy is all around us in every direction.... I do hope you have good crops and plenty of vegetables to eat. I wish I was with you to enjoy it. Tell my dear Mother to put up plenty of pickles, if I ever get home I will do them justice."[45]

The diary and letters of Asbury Speer could be, at best, merely another heart-rending tale of the horrors of the Civil War. But his story encompasses more than that. Attention must be paid to the uniqueness of Yadkin County, where the Quaker religion gripped the conscience of its people and a Whig majority balked at notions of Southern independence.

Adding further to the uniqueness of Asbury's tale is the Speer family itself. For a backwoods country family, living in the foothills of western North Carolina, the Speers were diverse and well educated, especially the women. In 1858, Asbury's sister, Annis Melissa Speer, wrote a long soliloquy that bears an uncanny resemblance to Asbury's poem written six years later. In many ways, she was a prophet, foreseeing her own fate and predicting the reunion of her family on the "other side." The essay she wrote was published in a Methodist newspaper shortly after her death. Certainly her words reflect the spirit of the romantic age, but they also represent the unshakable faith expressed in Asbury's poem, "The Dying Soldier."

The inscription on the gravestone of Annis Speer reads, "The Lord has answered my prayer in sparing me till the flowers of spring have come." She is buried beside Asbury on Cemetery Hill.

The Dream of Annis M. Speer
One Month Before Her Death

On last night, I had a dream, or a vision, which made me forget earth and all its pleasures. I dreamed I was in a strange place, where I saw a narrow passage that shined with exceeding brilliancy, and my brother and sister came and stood near me. And I

---

[45]Asbury Speer to father and mother, July 5, 1864 (Speer Family Papers).

saw God, and He blest me; and I gazed along the shining way, and longed to go up;—but God withdrew from my gaze, and my sister said: "Come with me;" but I lingered, I would fain go up. But they said, "Not yet," and we entered a strange doorway—into a wide open space resembling a meadow. It was perfectly level and completely matted over with the richest green grass. O! It looked like a fairy region. I asked, "Where are we?" They said, "This is Elysian fields;"—and they led on to a stream of water so clear and sparkling as though ten thousand diamonds were dancing on its surface. And my brother told me to drink;—and I drank;—and he told me to go in and wash;—and I plunged into its shining waves, and a thrill of delight—such as I never experienced in life before—possessed my whole frame. And I discovered, while I washed, my sister had left me—but my brother sat on the green grass a short distance from me. After a little while my sister came with a basket in her hand, and she told me the Great Father had prepared and sent me a new spring garment. And she dressed me—O! It was white and glittering—such as adorned her own saint-like form. And I looked about me—and I saw at a distance groups of shining forms, all dressed in purest white. And I asked who those creatures could be. They said, "They are angels—redeemed spirits—who are now triumphing over death and sin." And while we conversed—for we had been long parted, and we were now rejoicing together—I heard a strain of sweet melody—it was the evening hymn of the Redeemed! And they came nearer and nearer—and hailed me into their happy circle! O, joy—joy! I was safe in God's Kingdom! And just then, to my utter sorrow, I awoke![46]

Annis Melissa Speer, teacher and published writer, died April 23, 1858, at the age of 23.

---

[46]The dream of Annis M. Speer was published in the <u>North Carolina Christian Advocate</u>, Raleigh. There was no date on the clipping.

Assignments of the 28th Regiment

The 28th Regiment, North Carolina Troops, was assigned to the following commands and departments:

District of Cape Fear, Department of North Carolina (October 1861-March 1862).

Branch's Brigade, District of the Pamlico, Department of North Carolina (March 1862).

Branch's Brigade, Department of North Carolina (April-May 1862).

Branch's Brigade, Department of Northern Virginia (May 1862).

Branch's Brigade, A. P. Hill's Division, Army of Northern Virginia (May-June 1862).

Branch's Brigade, A. P. Hill's Division, Army of Northern Virginia (June-July 1862).

Branch-Lane's Brigade, A. P. Hill's Division, Jackson's 2nd Corps, Army of Northern Virginia (July 1862-May 1863).

Lane's Brigade, Pender-Wilcox's Division, A. P. Hill's 3rd Corps, Army of Northern Virginia (May 1863-April 1865).

Timeline 1861-1862

August 13, 1861 ....Asbury enlists in the Confederate army.

September 1861 ....Asbury's company is entertained by citizens of Salem and Winston, N. C.

September 1861..........28th Regiment N. C. Troops is organized at High Point, N. C., and James Henry Lane is elected Colonel.

March 19, 1862 ....Colonel Lane orders Asbury to return to Yadkin County and "enlist a sufficient number of recruits to raise his company to its maximum organization."

April 28, 1862 ....Asbury returns to the 28th Regiment at Kinston, N. C.

May 27, 1862 ....Asbury is taken prisoner at the Battle of Hanover Court House.

May 30, 1862 ....Prisoners arrive at Fort Monroe, Va.

June 2, 1862 ....Prisoners arrive in New York and are taken to Fort Columbus.

June 6, 1862 ....Asbury is given clothes by members of the Masonic order of New York.

June 16, 1862 ....Order is given to move the prisoners to Sandusky, Ohio.

June 21, 1862 ....Prisoners arrive at Johnson's Island on Lake Erie.

June 30, 1862 ....Prisoners receive news of the victory in the Seven Days Battles around Richmond, Va.

August 8, 1862 ....A prisoner is shot and killed on his way to bed.

September 1, 1862......Order is given to send the prisoners to Vicksburg, Miss., in a prisoner exchange. Three months pass before Asbury's next letter is written.

November 1, 1862 ......Asbury is promoted to Major.

December 13, 1862 ....The Battle of Fredericksburg is fought.

Battles in Which Colonel Speer
Was a Participant

William H. Asbury Speer participated in the following battles:

New Bern, North Carolina (March 14, 1862)

Hanover Court House, Virginia (May 27, 1862), taken prisoner
(Asbury was a Prisoner of War from May 27, 1862 to September 1, 1862)

Fredericksburg, Virginia (December 13, 1862)

Chancellorsville, Virginia (May 1-4, 1863), wounded

Gettysburg, Pennsylvania (July 1-3, 1863), wounded

Falling Waters, Virginia (July 10, 1863)

Bristoe Campaign (October-November 1863)

Bristoe Station, Virginia (October 14, 1863)

Mine Run Campaign (November-December 1863)

The Wilderness (May 5-6, 1864)

Spotsylvania Court House, Virginia (May 8-21, 1864)

North Anna (river) (May 22-26, 1864)

Cold Harbor, Virginia (June 1-3, 1864)

Gravel Hill, Virginia (July 28, 1864)

Fussell's Mill, Virginia (August 16, 1864)

Reams' Station (August 25, 1864), mortally wounded

Asbury Speer died August 29, 1864.

Diary and Letters
1861-1862

Camp Fisher, High Point, September 21, 1861

Lieutenant-Colonel James H. Lane:

Dear Sir,—You were unanimously elected Colonel of the Twenty-eighth North Carolina Volunteers this evening. This regiment is composed of the following companies enlisted for twelve months:

Co. A, Surry County, Captain Reeves (Major elect).
Co. B, Gaston County, Captain Edwards.
Co. C, Catawba County, Captain Lowe, (Lieutenant-
    Colonel elect).
Co. D, Stanly County, Captain Montgomery.
Co. E, Montgomery County, Captain Barringer.
Co. F, Yadkin County, Captain Kinyoun.
Co. G, Orange County, Captain Martin.
Co. H, Cleveland County, Captain Wright.
Co. I, Yadkin County, Captain Speer.
Co. K, Stanly County, Captain Moody.

You will see that most of us are 'Mountain Boys,' and we trust that we do not disgrace the home from which we come. It would afford us great pleasure and satisfaction to have for our leader an officer so well and favorably known for bravery, courtesy and professional attainments as Lieutenant-Colonel Lane, of the gallant 'Bethel' regiment. Permit us to express our personal hope that we may receive a favorable reply as soon as possible and to subscribe ourselves.

Your obedient servants,
    S. M. Stowe, Major Commanding Post
    Wm. J. Montgomery, Captain Co. D.
    G. B. Johnston, First Lieut. Co. G.
    Committee in behalf of the Twenty-eighth Regiment.[1]

---

[1]"The History of Lane's North Carolina Brigade," in <u>Southern Historical Society Papers</u>, Vol. 10 (1882), pp. 244-245, hereafter cited as <u>SHSP</u>.

Wilmington Nov 27th 1861

Dear Mother,

I wrote to you a few days ago that I was unwell and would write to you again soon.... I have been very unwell; was quite sick but I am much better & will be well & stout in a day or two I hope. I was so glad to see the boys. You cannot imagine how proud I was to see them—it did me great good to see them. I was very glad to get your kind and affectionate letter. I read it with tears in my eyes, for it waked up all the feelings of childhood, when I used to be a little boy, & listened to those lessons of Motherly advice & religious lessons. I am fully aware of the sorrows and troubles you see about me & I do most certainly appreciate all those feelings of parental affections. I think of you often both day & night, but dear Mother, I do not want you to see too much trouble about me. For you have seen so much trouble about your children, who are better [off] than you & I. For I will, my dear Mother, do the best I can to avoid disease & to preserve my health.

Also I will do all I can to take care of myself both in battle as well as out of it. I have plenty of good head clothes [caps] to keep me warm in any sort of weather, but I am very often taking cold—as well as all the other men have had colds. We cough very much, but my men are much better off than they have been. I feel resigned to my fate. I am fully of opinions that I will get back home safe to see you all. I am fully of a notion I will come home about New Year. Give my love to dear old Aunt & Pappy and all of you. Pray for me & I will pray for myself. May God bless you. Write to me often.

Your son, W. H. A. Speer

I send a receipt to you by Vet for $175 which I want you to keep for me till my time is out, which receipt I paid that money to him today. I want Papa or him or James to use if they need it.

Head Quarters 28th Regt. NC Vols.
Kinston N. C. March 19th 1862

Special Order

No._____

Capt. W. H. A. Speer of Co. I, 28th N. C. Volunteers is hereby detailed as recruiting officer. He will proceed without delay to Yadkin County where his company was raised, and there enlist a sufficient number of recruits to raise it to its maximum organization.

James H. Lane
Co. Command. 28th Regt. N. C. Vols.

Kinston April 28/62

Dear Father

I arrived here last night or on yesterday arriving all safe. I had to lay over at High Point one night. There are five Regts. of infantry encamped in the same field. Kinston is a very pretty place. We are in sight [of it]—¾ mile off. My men are all gone on picket duty—only the recruits in camp. They were very glad to see me. I have no news towards or about New Bern[2]—only our pickets are having some engagements. New Orleans is now in the hands of the enemy—so [the] report says. It is believed, if that is the case, we are in a bad row for stumps. If that is the case we will ultimately be subjugated either by their arms or from farming in salt.[3]

I feel as well as I did when I left home, only I am sorty sore from traveling. All the way from Goldsburrow [Goldsboro] there is nearly one military camp and, [in] Raleigh, there are between 12,000 to 15,000 men & I tell you it looks like starvation will come upon the country. Bacon is worth 30 cts. by the retail & scarce at that. I will write more in a few days. I shall ever remember all your kindness to me while at home. My mother's great care for me will ever be remembered by

---

[2]New Bern was captured by Federal General Ambrose Burnside on March 14, 1862.
[3]When the Romans defeated the Carthaginians, salt was plowed into the soil so nothing would grow.

me. Hoping you are all well & sending my respects & love to you all & hoping to see you all safe again—I am your son,

W. H. A. Speer

Write when convenient. Tell Dr. Dozier his boys[4] are both well & very glad to see me.

Dr. Nathan B. Dozier (1823-1874)
Dr. Dozier named the town of Boonville, N. C. His two sons, Smith and Nathan C., served in Asbury's company (I) from Yadkin County. Dr. Dozier's daughter, Selena Francis, married Asbury's brother James. Dr. Dozier is my great great great grandfather.

Selena Francis Dozier Speer (1848-1941)
Asbury's sister-in-law Selena Speer, wife of James Speer, is my great great grandmother.

---

[4]Dr. Nathan B. Dozier's sons, Smith and Nathan C., served in Asbury's company. Asbury's brother James married Selena Frances Dozier, daughter of Dr. Nathan B. Dozier. Dr. Dozier is my great great great grandfather.

[In May of 1862, as McClellan's Army moved slowly up the peninsula toward Richmond, Branch's Brigade was ordered to Hanover Court House to guard the railroad and protect the flank of the Confederate Army against attack from Fredericksburg. On May 27, Branch, being outnumbered three to one, was overwhelmed by the Vth Corps under command of General Fitz John Porter.[5] The following are diary entries made by W. H. A. Speer during this period.]

I was taken prisoner at the battle of Hanover C[ourt] H[ouse], Va. May 27, 1862 & with our Regt. & Brigade was on the way to Richmond from Hanover C. H. [We] camped about 5 miles from Hanover C. H. on the night of 26th of May. We had a very rainy night which made the mud deep the next morning. We all suffered much that night as we had no tents, neither had we slept in tents but one night in five weeks, traveling all the time in mud & rain. I & Lieut. Bohannon went to a ____ house in the night and got our supper & there we met up with Capts. Eperson[6] [Apperson] & Lowe[7] and various others. We got a good supper & how glad [I would have been] if my poor hungry men could have been along to [have] took part of it. In the morning (the 27), I was ordered to detail men from my company to assist Captain Latham with his battery. We were then ordered into line of battle (our Regt. the 28th N. C.). We then was ordered to return back to the road towards Hanover Court House. In obeying the order we passed through our entire Brigade. As we passed some of our men close to the R.R. [railroad], they told us we would be certain to ketch a fight that day. The road was very muddy. Some places almost impossible for the men to travel & one place we had to leave the road. We finally come to Dr. Kinney's house two & half or three miles from camp, where we halted in a little old field till ten men from each company

---

[5]Mark M. Boatner III, Civil War Dictionary (New York: David McKay Company, Inc., 1988), p. 373, hereafter cited as Boatner's Dictionary.

[6]Thomas Apperson was elected Captain in Company F, "the Yadkin Boys," of the 28th Regiment on April 12, 1862. He resigned because of ill health on January 26, 1865. N. C. Troops, Vol. VIII, p. 174.

[7]Thomas Lowe, from Catawba County, served as Captain in Company C of the 28th Regiment. He died of fever on June 10, 1862. N. C. Troops, Vol. VIII, p. 139.

Thomas Apperson
Elected Captain in Company F, "The Yadkin Boys," of the 28th Regiment N.C.T. on April 12, 1862. He resigned because of ill health on January 26, 1865. (Photo from Clark, N. C. Regiments, 1901.)

went to Dr. Kinney's well & filled all the canteens full of water. While we were there in the old field the enemy was in 40 yards of us, hiding in a pine thicket to our right, but they did not fire on us, neither did we then see them (but I was told that night that they were there).

At Dr. Kinney's house we took the right hand & went down the road to a mill on the Pamunkey River. We halted in a lane above the hill & loaded our guns & waited there till our scouts reported that the enemy was flanking us, which was a mistake as it afterwards proved to be two companies of our Brigade on picket. This I am certain in as they came to us in the fight. We then faced to the left & went back up the road toward Dr. Kinney's house by the left flank. We placed Capt. G. B. Johnston[8] of Co. G on the right of the road in a piece of woods with 20 of his men as skirmishers, & just as we were filing around by the left into the old field at Dr. Kinney's, our left flank was fired upon [by] the 25th New York, that was then in line of battle in the apple orchard of Dr. Kinney's on the left of the house. At the same time we were also fired upon by the 5th Mass. who had been deployed upon our left in the pine thickets (before named) as skirmishers. Thus, we were exposed to a direct fire in front & also a fire from the thicket on our left. This was an entire surprise to all of us, as we had no intelligence of the enemy being in that place or near there. We were taken entirely by surprise. Our men never faltered at the heavy fire of the enemy. We were ordered to about face, by companies, half wheel through the woods which was done by all the companies except Capt. Montgomery[9] & Capt. Epperson [Apperson] who did not march through the woods as was ordered. They marched up the road to where the fight commenced. The other companies marched through the woods driving the skirmishers through

---

[8]G. B. Johnston, from Orange County, served as Captain in Company G of the 28th Regiment. N. C. Troops, Vol. VIII, pp. 184-185. "He was the life of the prison on Johnson's Island, though rapidly nearing death with consumption, and used to read the Episcopal service to his fellow-prisoners every Sunday. He used to tell them that he never knew how to appreciate his prayer-book, especially the litany, until he was himself a prisoner and invoked God's 'pity upon all prisoners and captives.'" SHSP, Vol. 18, pp. 132-133.
[9]William J. Montgomery, from Stanly County, served as Captain in Company O of the 28th Regiment. N. C. Troops, Vol. VIII, p. 158.

Nicholas Gibbon

Captain, Company I (Yadkin County), 28th Regiment N.C.T. Nicholas Gibbon was the brother of Union General John Gibbon. (Photo from Clark, N. C. Regiments, 1901.)

Ed Lovell

Promoted to Captain of Company A (Surry County) of the 28th Regiment N.C.T. on April 9, 1862. He survived the war and later settled in Boone, N. C., where many of his descendants live today. (Photo from Clark, N. C. Regiments, 1901.)

the woods. We came upon them in companies. The left of my company fired one full volley as we came upon them killing & wounding 10 at once. About the same time Capt. Lovell's[10] men was firing in the woods to my left very heavy. About this time Capt. Gibbon's[11] horse came dashing by me riderless. I first thought it was Col. Lane's, and was fearful he was killed, but afterwards found I was mistaken, much to my gratification. Our advance was much hindered by the underbrush. Capt. Gibbon passed in front of my company just before he was thrown from his horse. He was quite cool & was encouraging the men to keep cool. Capt. Lovell & his men acted very bravely in the woods.

As we came into the road from the woods in the rear, we were in front of the line of battle formed by the enemy at the commencement of the fight. By the time we got into the road the enemy was in retreat across the wheat field. Our men then broke across the plank fence & through the wheat after the Yankees. Our men crossed into the center of the wheat field & then we were ordered by someone to fall back to the edge of the woods on the side of the road. As well as I recollect, Capt. Lovell on my left & Capt. Linebarger[12] on my right & my company in the center fell back to the woods. As we crossed over the plank fence into the road we saw one Regt. of the enemy coming up the road in our rear. Our men sprang into the woods & a brisk fire was commenced by file upon the Regt. then advancing in our rear. The fire was commenced by Capt. Lovell's men and extended through my company & I think through Capt. Linebarger's.

The enemy was in sixty yds. of us when the fire commenced. Our fire was very heavy & had the good effect of driving the enemy back. We killed many of the enemy down the road at that time, as I know having seen in the road next

---

[10]Ed Lovell, from Surry County, was promoted to Captain in Company A of the 28th Regiment on April 9, 1862. He survived the war and later settled in the Boone, North Carolina, area. N. C. Troops, Vol. VIII, p. 112.

[11]Nicholas Gibbon, brother of Union General John Gibbon, was Captain of Commissary in Company I of the 28th Regiment. Another brother, Robert, served as surgeon in Company I. N. C. Troops, Vol. VIII, p. 111.

[12]James Linebarger, from Catawba County, served as Captain in Company C of the 28th Regiment. He was wounded at Fredericksburg, Chancellorsvile, and Gettysburg. He was present when Lee surrendered to Grant on April 9, 1865. N. C. Troops, Vol. VIII, p. 139.

James Linebarger
Served as Captain in Company C (Catawba County) of the 28th Regiment N.C.T. He was wounded at Fredericksburg, Chancellorville, and Gettysburg. He was present when Lee surrendered at Appomattox on April 9, 1865. (Photo from Clark, N. C. Regiments, 1901.)

Simon S. Bohannon
Served as Lieutenant of Company I (Yadkin County) in the 28th Regiment N.C.T. He was present when Lee surrendered at Appomattox on April 9, 1865. Several members of his family are buried at the Speer farm on Cemetery Hill. (Photo from Clark, N. C. Regiments, 1901.)

morning much sign of blood & the enemy admitted that the fire was severe on them.

Their bullets passed principally over our heads, as we had no man killed in the road. I had one man, Headspeth, shot through the hand; my men through all this time acted very bravely. My Lieuts., Bohannon[13] & Long,[14] was quite cool & determined marching in front of my company exerting all their powers to keep the men quiet & showing them how to aim & fire deliberately while in the woods in the [front?] part of the engagement. I seen the Adjutant of the enemy Regt. killed. He was shot off of his horse by one of Capt. Linebarger's men.

As is supposed, all this time the enemy were throwing shot & shell from their batteries at us but doing but little damage. We were ordered to advance into the wheat field again, which we did, passing directly under the artillery fire of the enemy. We advanced beyond the center of the wheat field where our Regt. was formed. We then marched by the right flank out into the pasture field of Dr. Kinney's where we were thrown into columns of companies and marched by Lieut. Col. Lowe[15] to the top of a hill on the spring in the same field. As we were marching in this direction a shell passed so near my head I dodged to one side & came very near falling, the shell striking the flagbearer & a private in Company C just before & knocking both of them down. We were halted by Col. Lowe on the hill & marched back close to where our two little cannon were placed & had opened fire on the enemy's guns.

Prior to this Capt. G. B. Johnston of Co. G was ordered to take 20 of his men & go out upon our left & see if he could ascertain the position & force of the enemy, a very important order to be complied with; but it could not have been entrusted to any Capt. and his men, who would have accom-

[13]Neal and Simon Bohannon served as Lieutenants in Company I of the 28th Regiment. Neal died of fever on June 20, 1863. Simon survived the war. N. C. Troops, Vol. VIII, p. 207.

[14]Frederick Long, from Yadkin County, served in Company I of the 28th Regiment. He died at Winchester, Virginia, on October 23, 1862. N. C. Troops, Vol. VIII, p. 207.

[15]When James Henry Lane became brigade commander in the fall of 1862, Samuel Lowe was promoted to Colonel of the 28th Regiment. He was wounded at Gettysburg on July 3, 1863. N. C. Troops, Vol. VIII, p. 110.

plished the object any better. It is proper here to state that this accounts perhaps for him & his men being taken prisoner, as we had left the field on the retreat before he came back & he was not aware that the Regt. was retreating until he came back.

Capt. Stowe[16] previous to this was ordered with his company to take their position to the left of the battery to support the artillery & to hold his position, which was a very dangerous one, as well as important. But he was & is well qualified to fill such a position with his brave company.

While we were maneuvering in the field I seen a shell strike a young Mr. Roberts of Co. A [Pleasant H. Roberts of Surry County, North Carolina] injuring him badly fracturing both of his thighs from which he died. Also I seen two more men of Co. A killed with shells, taking off the top of one of their heads & cutting the other [in two].

We left the top of the hill before named & formed our line in rear of our guns. From there we seen the enemy to our right coming out of the woods as if to flank us. Col. Lane ordered us to deploy along a fence to the right & lay down behind the fence, which we did. And we were ordered then as the enemy seemed not inclined to attack us there but to keep still on their flank movement. We were ordered to deploy along the fence to the right & cross the branch below the spring.

Here I left Lieut. Bohannon, who was now broke down. He was sick & had been sick for some days. I was sorry to leave him for he had acted bravely all the fight but could go no longer. As we passed along the swamp & over the field I seen several men who had give out & was lying down exhausted with heat & fatigue.

After crossing the branch we filed down the branch to see if we could ascertain as to the enemy's whereabouts. Capt. Montgomery was ordered to send some of his men down into the woods to look after the enemy. They started & about this time Maj. Lowe came riding down where we were & told us we

<hr/>

[16]Samuel Stowe, from Gaston County, was appointed Major in the 28th Regiment on April 16, 1863. N. C. Troops, Vol. VIII, p. 110.

were ordered to retreat. He was quite cool & had acted very bravely all day. We faced about and passed up the hollow into the main road to Hanover C. H. In going this route we had to pass directly under the fire of the enemy's guns. I only seen one man killed on this route. He was a man of Co. H.

By the time I got up to the road I was entirely broke down & thought I could go no further but the idea of having passed safely through the fight & then falling in the hands of the enemy spurred me on. There were some 70 of my men then with [me]. I had fell behind in getting out of the field. The remainder of my company was on before with Lieut. Long. While we were passing along the road by Mr. Winston's the minnie balls came thick & fast after us striking the fence on all sides of us with their deathly whistle. Also the shells at this time was following us with their awful death howl, bursting over our heads & striking the ground & throwing the dirt over us.

By this time our artillery came dashing by. I then thought of Capt. Stowe who was left behind. Not until then was he aware of the retreat, having stayed at his post with his men under the fire of the enemy's guns, much exposed. This accounts for his being captured. Now the retreat had freely commenced, but before I go further, while we were in the field of battle & our guns were belching forth shell & shot at the enemy, Col. Lane seen a white flag held up by the enemy. He immediately ordered firing to be stopped & sent a man ahead with a white handkerchief upon his gun. But directly we heard their guns again and here came the deathly shells through the air—one struck a smokehouse & exploded in the house shattering everything. One other at the same time cut off the top of a large rake in the yard. Although this was the first fight we had been in, our men acted bravely. We held the field as long as we could. Having been in the fight three hours & fifteen minutes, many of our men were entirely broke down as we had marched through the mud up to our shoe tops & from that to half leg deep all the morning.

Our officers all acted coolly & brave. Col. Lane was as cool and composed as if we had been only on a battalion drill.

My men never will show any more bravery than on that day. My Lieuts. were very cool & acted with as much bravery as old soldiers. Lieut. Long is deserving of much credit for his conduct. I cannot praise my men & officers as well as they deserve. But here comes the doleful tale.

We continued our retreat to Hanover C. H. where we halted for a short time. In going there I gave my knapsack to Lieut. Randle[17] of Co. D as he had got a artillery horse to ride. As I went on I passed many of my men & men of the Regt. who had fell down & could go no further—poor fellows left behind to be picked up by the enemy who now was in full pursuit of us. We got to the court house. I told Col. Lane I could go no further. He said I must go as far as I could.

I here seen Lieut. Long who came to me. He was glad to see me. I told him I did not think I could go but [a] little further. He was in hopes I could hold out. While here we seen the enemy in pursuit of us. We then commenced our retreat. About this time we heard the attack of our Brigade in the rear of the enemy. The cannonading was very heavy. We were then in hopes the enemy would stop the pursuit, but we were now sadly mistaken. We heard our little gun fire back at the court house in our rear. The fire was made at the enemy's cavalry. This was hardly over before here come our gunners, horses & cavalry men rushing along the road crying to us "all to clear the road." This created quite a stampede among our men as we were confident that the enemy's cavalry was just behind, as many of, & I may say, all of the men behind the Regt. broke into the woods & went some distance from the road.

I went but a short distance from the road & soon got back into the road seeing it was our own men when we got into the road. At the end of the lane it was near a half mile across the river bottom to the bridge. We pushed on & tried to gain the bridge, but it was impossible to do it as the enemy's cavalry was now just behind us. I filed off to the right in a wheat field. As I did this I looked back & seen many of our broke

---

[17]John Randle, from Stanly County, was promoted to Captain of Company D of the 28th Regiment on May 2, 1863. He died on July 10, 1863, from wounds received at Gettysburg. N. C. Troops, Vol. VIII, p. 153.

down men behind in every direction, slipping through the wheat doing all they could to get out of the way of the enemy. Our Regt. was then in sight on a high hill over a mile ahead of us on the opposite side of the river. I had no hopes of overtaking our Regt. I, with a small party of 15 men, made for the riverbank. When we got there we found it very deep & much wider than I expected. [I] seen there was no chance for us to cross. I could have swam the river but my men could not & they begged me to stay with them. With tears in their eyes, [they] told me they had stuck by me all day & would have died around me to have saved my life. How could I then leave such men?

I contented myself to stay and seal my fate with them. We were in hopes we would yet be rescued. But Alas! As the sun was setting & its last bright rays were kissing the tops of the trees, on came the furious cavalry charging upon us, to whom we had to surrender, or be destroyed, as there were only 15 of us & 60 of them [and] just at [the] river & over 1,000 in sight. Here I had the most awful feelings I ever have had in my life. Thousands of thoughts came rushing through my mind & I almost wished I was back on the field of battle lying with my comrades in the cold embrace of death.

We were now five miles from the battlefield, to which place we were marched. As we got into the road I came up with other prisoners of my company & the Regt. It was a tiring time. [We were] all broke down, but we had to drag along even at the point of the bayonet. As we marched back to the battleground our number increased. I passed Hanover & went back the road that we came.

We finally got back to Dr. Kinney's house where the battle commenced. It was now dark, but O! how the place was changed. The enemy was camped in every direction with all the implements of war and [I] wondered how it was that we had escaped as long as we did or how it was that any of the Regt. was not all taken or killed. Our number was taken. The privates were marched to the stables where they had other prisoners & put under strong guards. I was taken with some other officers to Genl. Butterfield[18] where I was asked several questions as to the fight. [I was asked] about the Union sentiment in N. C., all of which I had some fun in answering. I was paroled & sent over to Col. Lancing's quarters.

As I went over there I had to pass through the army all the way. On arriving at Lancing's quarters, I found Lieut. Bohannon & Maj. Lowe of our Regt. prisoners. Here I ascertained all about the fight in the evening with our Brigade— also our fight in the morning. Our Regt., the 28th N. C., was opposed in the morning by 3 brigades before we left the field. I ascertained from them that the 25th N. Y. Regt. was badly cut up—[they were] the first regt. we engaged. The next was the 44th N. Y., which was badly hurt, the 5th Mass. was damaged badly. The 6th Penn., who was the skirmishers, was hurt badly in the skirmish fight. The fight in the evening with our Brigade was very destructive to us as well as the enemy.

I passed a retched night upon the cold wet ground. A little oil cloth under me was all I had to keep me off the wet ground & mud. I had nothing to cover with. I was very cold all night, having sweated myself nearly to death. I was not even dry next day till the sun dried me off. I was so tired my limbs ached, so I could not sleep. I longed to see day come. I went to a sentinel fire in the night to warm. The moon was then in full blaze & the whole field was covered with the sleeping soldiers, horses, cannon, & ambulances. I could hear the ambulances still traveling, bringing in the wounded, a solemn sight and a sight for meditation & thought. Morning came & with it the sight of the destruction of the day before. I went with the other prisoners over to Genl. Porter's[19] quarters at Kenny's house. When I got there I beheld an awful sight—the houses, corncrib, shuck pen, wagon & yard full of wounded, with their cries & moanings from the affect of wounds & the surgeon's knife & here & there lay a poor soldier who had expired during the night. I am not able to paint

---

[18]Daniel Butterfield led the Third Brigade of the Union Army during the Peninsular Campaign.
[19]Fitz John Porter commanded the Vth Corps of the U. S. Army at the Battle of Hanover Court House, where the Branch Brigade was overwhelmed by superior numbers.

the horrible scene here witnessed by me & I hope never to see it again.

I now learned the strength of Genl. Porter's corps. It was over 20,000 men with 2,000 cavalry & 72 pieces of cannon. No wonder we were whipped—I here counseled Porter, who is chief in command—the other levels under him there were Reynolds, McCall, Morrell, Jones, Brooks, and Butterfield. Here I got a good account of the fight. I found certain we had 18 killed in the 28th Reg. & 15 men wounded that was in the enemy's hand. The enemy had over 1,000 wounded at Kenny's from the two fights that day, besides what they had at 3 other places. They had wounded on the other side of the field.

[I] supposed in all, from the best accts [accounts], I could get 1800 wounded. As to our loss I can only now guess, but it was heavy in killed & wounded; prisoners taken 500 in all. The enemy's loss was much more than was stated by them, as I seen more dead myself than they accounted for. I passed over about half of the battleground where the fight was in the evening & the destruction was terrible on both sides—dead men, horses, broken wagons, ambulances, gun carriages— the timber tore all to pieces & ground busted up—everywhere destruction was visible in every direction.

So ended the Hanover fight. I might have mentioned many interesting circumstances connected with this fight but have not done so. Now, I only have give a short account of what came under my own attention. Many other things occurred which I did not see. I will here say I was taken by Capt. C. J. Whitney 5th U.S. Cavalry—he also was captured before Richmond and is now a prisoner.

May the 28, 1862
8 o'clock P.M.

All of us prisoners were now drawn up in a line in the road before Dr. Kenny's house. It was a long line of Rebels, over 300. We were here informed that we were to be sent to Genl.

McClellan's[20] headquarters—18 miles. We started off in a long, sad-looking line. We passed by a part of the battlefield where they were burying the dead on both sides. I seen 50 of our men all in one pile by the side of a large hole dug to bury them in. The N. Y. Zouaves[21] were very busy pillaging their pockets after their money, pocket knives and other little tricks. I felt sorry for these poor men far from home and friends.

As we marched along the road we were continually meeting troops, Regts., Brigades. Artillery after artillery was hurrying on with numerous cavalry & every now and then we would pass long lines of baggage wagons, sections of them drawn by the best horses and mules I ever seen. On we went and on came McClellan's hosts. It was terrible to suffer the thought of what was before our men. Such equipments for the destruction of men I never had seen before. It was now 12 o'clock and we had come to a halt to rest. Our men were now very tired. The day was very warm and some of the men were already now giving out. We were guarded by a cavalry company. Some of them were very kind to us.

We were not allowed long to take our ease. We soon were ordered up and on the march again. The road in some places was very muddy. In some places we had to wade in mud and water up to our boot tops, all the time meeting soldiers, baggage wagons and passing their camps. The country on all sides bore plain marks of the invader's destruction, fences thrown down burnt and crops turned out. We seen but very few citizens. We are now opposite a place, [a] fine residence, and a yard is placed around the house. Here a cavalry man took my canteen and rode out to a well and got me a canteen of water. When he came back he offered me a drink of good whiskey, which you know I took a hearty one. In a short

---

[20]General George McClellan commanded the U. S. Army during the Seven Days Battles of the Peninsular Campaign in June of 1862.

[21]The 5th New York Volunteers, Duryee's Zouaves, favored the colorful dress of French North African troops, the Zouaves. This uniform was usually comprised of a short jacket and waistcoat, a broad sash, baggy pantaloons, gaiters, and a tassled fez. The South also had its "Zouaves," such as the famous Louisiana Tigers from New Orleans who fought at First Bull Run. For picture, see John MacDonald, Great Battles of the Civil War (New York: Macmillan Publishing Co), 1988, pp. 14-15.

time he offered me his horse to ride. I was glad to get the chance for I was near giving out. It was 5 miles from here to camp. This cavalry man was an Irishman. He let me ride his horse to camp. We now passed 2 Regts. of infantry, with 4 batteries (24 pieces cannon and six of the celebrated coffee-mill guns). They throw sixty balls in a minute and I took a good look at them. The enemy told me they had several of them in their army.

We were soon in a mile of camp. The Yankee soldiers were now on all sides of the road to get a good look at the dirty rebels. We were gazed and stared at as if we had been live Devils and they were nearly as fearful of us. Many of our men had give out and had to ride. We were now in sight of McClellan's camp. We could see them forming their lines to march us into camp. Every man far and near was now on stretch as hard as his legs could carry him to see the rebels. We were marched under heavy guard into camp where we were halted and our names, rank, and Regt. was taken by the federal officers. The heavy guard could hardly keep the outsiders off. They seemed to be amazed to see that we were human beings as same as themselves. Many odd remarks were made as to our looks and dress. We all enjoyed it very well to think men belonging to the grand army of the U. S. had men who was as ignorant as they were. This satisfied us. If the mere appearance of the Rebels without arms did so much to excite the Yanks, what would they think of doing when they come in contact with our boys with their guns—just run as a matter of getting away. After our names were taken, we were put then into a bull pen and a double guard put over us, who were very ill to us.

We were now almost starved to death, not having had anything to eat in 36 hours. [We] slept one night in the rain without any tents, marched and fought all day, [were] taken prisoner, slept on the cold, wet ground, and then marched 18 miles over some of the worst road in the world, without anything to eat. [This] made us feel much like eating. We soon had plenty of crackers and fresh beef issued to us and all hands went to cooking. Some of the men were so hungry they eat the beef raw as though it was the best diet in the world. We were all soon done cooking and eating and down upon the cold ground to sleep, as though it was the best bed in the world.

Morning came May 29, a beautiful morning. We all got our breakfast soon. We were hardly done eating before it was announced another large lot of prisoners had arrived. All of us Rebs were anxious to see them. So we soon had the pleasure and found they were of our Regts. and Brigades. Our number now was increased to 500. We were now put under march for the White House Landing,[22] 16 miles [away]. We only had 8 miles to walk to dispatch station where we were to take the train for the White House. We were guarded by infantry today, who treated us very kindly, but such a crowd of heathens. As we passed through today it is proper to say they were volunteers and not Regulars. We passed many soldiers today and had all kind of abuse heaped upon us on all sides. Whenever we passed by a camp it was a general rush to the road side and then we would get hard names thrust at us, such as G. D. dirty rebels, Rebel cut throats, you ought to be hung, have your throats cut, burnt, etc. No one would give us the credit of being humans; [we] did not have horns nor tails but, damn them, they are Rebels.

We arrived at Dispatch Station at one o'clock and took the cars for the White House. We were all very tired and glad to get on the iron horse wagons again. We soon got to the White House Landing, where we were received by a very strong guard with the finger of derision pointed at us, and to mend the matter, here we found the plagued nigger[23] coming up making mouths at us—if we were not worth any other kind of notice—and winked at by the Yanks. Thinks I, you will soon find something else to wink at, when you see our boys' muskets and cannon blazing away at you. The river, he is wide and deep. It was full of transports, gun boats and vessels of all kinds. We had passed through a once beautiful

---

[22]White House Landing, strategically located on the Pamunkey River, close to the Richmond Railroad, was briefly held by the Union army during the Peninsular Campaign.
[23]Asbury's parents did not own slaves and were opposed to slavery, yet it is obvious that, in Asbury's opinion, African-Americans should be subservient to whites.

rich country, but it is now entirely devastated and crops, fences, houses all ruined—the whole country looked like starvation.

We were marched upon a transport steamer Ariel for Fortress Monroe.[24] We steamed down the river about 5 o'clock. It was a very interesting time—every rebel full of curiosity. While at White House Landing we amused ourselves and the Yanks by selling them Confederate stamps, N. C. and Va. shinplaster [paper currency]. It was amusing to see how anxious they were to get our money to send to their friends and it suited us poor fellows for we had not a cent to buy anything with. We found some clever men who would go ashore and buy many things for us and bring to us. We travelled down the river [about] 25 miles, when a gun boat that was with us run aground, so we here waited for [a] day to get off again. I passed through the boat and the prisoners were all down everywhere asleep, so I looked out [for] as soft [a] plank as I could find, and down I tumble and slept soundly.

May 29

Up all hands soon this morning in want of something to eat, for we had had nothing to eat for 24 hours. We raised a general howl for bread and meat. About 7 o'clock we got some cold ham and crackers. During this time they were trying to get off the gun boat, which was accomplished in a short time by hitching a long rope to our vessel and dragging her off the bank.

Now all hands of us went steaming down the river at a rapid rate. We seen plenty to interest us today. [We] passed several places of note: West Point, where there was a battle fought, Yorktown noted in the war of 1776, as well as for various incidences of the present war.

This evening we had a heavy sea and had to put back into a small bay where we stayed all night. It was a stormy night but we all slept very soundly.

---

[24]Fort Monroe was located at the very tip of the Virginia peninsula.

May 30

This morning we sailed down to Fortress Monroe through a very thick fog. [We] got there at 6 o'clock P.M. This is quite a fort, a beautiful harbor. There were many transports in the harbor and quite a quantity of war materials on land. The _____ are in sight of here, also Hampton Roads. The college is the only thing that remains of the beautiful and ancient village of Hampton, which is in sight.

The destruction of the <u>Congress</u> and other vessels by the <u>Merrimac</u> are plain here to be seen. It was a great feat of the war. They seem yet to have a holy horror of the <u>Merrimac</u>.

We embarked on board of the steamer <u>Star of the South</u> for N. Y. We set sail about 11 o'clock P.M. <u>The Star of the South</u> is a beautiful sailing steamer. It was but a short time before we were out of sight of land, upon the beautiful blue waves of the great ocean. The prisoners were much interested in the ocean as many never seen it before. We had a beautiful day; calm sea. So we had nothing to excite us, only in fancying to ourselves what will become of us, [or] how we would be treated, if we would be exchanged or paroled, or perhaps we are to be shot or hung. While in this mood our attention would be drawn off by some large wave rushing to meet us as though it defied us to combat. The sea bird was flying in all directions, which was the only live thing then to be seen. As far as our eyes could reach, wave after wave seemed to be chasing off each other, bursting only to rise up in more gigantic power. To find upon the great ocean its splendid magnificent powers must impress us with the great and wonderful power of the great and good being.

It was now nearly night and supper was fixed for us, which was coffee, cold ham, and light bread. We all were very proud of our coffee, as we had got none in a long time. We were all very hungry and eat quite hasty. The officers eat in the cabin and had a good supper. Shortly after supper, O how sick we were now getting. Sea sick had got hold of nearly all of us and quite a settling of accounts now took place. Men were vomiting in every place almost—poor fellows—how sick they are. You never know what sick is till you are sea sick, then you realize it fully. It was now night and we all were tumbling down to sleep. I got on one of the seats at the table and slept finally. Our men on the lower deck had to sleep like hogs on the floor and in their companion's vomit. If you want to see hard times and do as you can just be a prisoner of war.

May 31

We were all rather sick this morning, had a hard day at sea, nothing to interest us today, only the looks of the great blue sea with its wave after wave still rushing after us.

Sunday, June 1

I slept last night on the floor in the cabin. This morning I feel better. I have been down among the boys. They all look badly—poor fellows—I wish they were all back in Dixie. This is Sunday, a beautiful day. If I was at home I could go to church, but no church on the steamer. The Yankee officers and soldiers all look clean and with boots all blacked up nice. O, what a contrast, [with] us poor dirty Seceshes [Secessionists] prisoners. No wonder they gaze at us—but we are the soldiers of liberty. The capt. of the steamer give us a good dinner today. This evening we have a rough sea. We all are now fixing to sleep. Some of us officers are on the floor, others on the seats, etc. Hope to wake up at N. Y. in the morning.

June 2

This morning finds us in sight of land one time more and now sailing up the bay into N. Y. harbor. We have plenty now to look at. Towns on both sides of us and here is a fort and there is another—Staten Island, Long Island on one side, with Jersey City, Hoboken, on one side, and Brooklyn on the other with the great city of N. Y. before us and Governor's Island, Castle William and Fort Columbus to our right. Now our steamer casts anchor and here comes the N. Y. Yankees to see the bloody Seceshes. "Look, Pa," says a very pretty little girl, "they have got no horns and tails as I can see. Where are they?" This expression of the innocent little girl goes to show fully what kind of training the Northern children receive from their parents.

We were taken off of the ship on to a little steamer and took to Governor's Island, where we landed under guard. Here we were separated from our privates. They were marched to Castle William where some 500 other prisoners were. The officers were all marched into Fort Columbus to our quarters, where we met several of our brother officers from N. C. We met our esteemed friend, Col. C. M. Avery,[25] the hero of the battle of New Bern, N. C., with the other N. C. officers who were taken there. Also, Col. Olmsted of Ga. and his officers surrendered at Fort Pulaski. Col. Avery and his officers, with our Ga. friends, all set themselves to work to fix us a good dinner, which we thankfully received, after which they give us plenty of clean, nice clothes to put on, giving us the chance to wash up and look like white folks. We certainly did need it, for of all the dirty fellows, we were certainly the dirtiest. The N. C. and Ga. officers were very kind to us, such kindness as only can be found in abundance in a pure Southern patriot's breast. We were shown our quarters by Provost Marshall Casy and beds were sent to us and by night we had our quarters cleaned out and fixed up well and was as comfortable as we did expect to be. I went down to see our privates all go into the castle. Here I seen 6 of my men that were taken at New Bern, N. C. We all came back to our quarters and took a good night's sleep.

June 3

I feel much refreshed this morning from a good night's sleep. After breakfast we assigned our parole and was shown our bounds, where we were allowed to go and no further. Col. Loomis is in command of this island and fort. He is an old Army officer, near sixty years of age. His hair and whiskers are very white. Governor's Island is as pretty [a] place as you possibly can imagine it to be. There are several families living on the Island, besides many inside of the fort. Col. Loomis and family, [along] with a high Episcopal Diocese's family, also live on the Island.

---

[25]Clark Moulton Avery first served as Captain in Company G of the 1st North Carolina Regiment. He later served as Colonel in the 33rd Regiment of James Henry Lane's Brigade. N. C. Troops, Vol. IX, p. 118.

Clark Moulton Avery
Avery first served as Captain, Company G, First Regiment, N.C.T. He
later served as Colonel, 33rd Regiment, N.C.T. Avery County, N. C.,
was named for the Avery family. (Photo from Clark, N. C. Regiments,
1901.)

There are several war accoutrements. Cannon cargoes are made here. There are 4 comps [companies] of infantry here acting as guards. They drill every morning and evening, which we frequently go to see and particularly to dress parade. This I cannot describe so as to interest you. Capt. Clinton commonly appears and takes command. He is unfortunately a very homely hard favored man but, by the way, quite a clever man. There is a fine brass band that discourses music for us every day. Mixed with this, we have the rattle of the drums and squealing of the fifes almost constantly.

Fort Columbus is a beautiful place inside as well as out, except on top of the fort. There are over 1,600 large cannon mounted, which does not look so pleasant from the outside of the fort. Within the fort here is almost one-half acre of land in a square, through the center of which passes the walk 10 feet wide from one sallie point to the other (the only two entrances into the fort). This is crossed at right angles by another walk 10 feet wide from the opposite side of the fort to the other. In the center of the lot is a fine well of water. All around the lot on each side is a large block of buildings 3 stories high. As quarters for officers and men in one of these blocks, we were quartered. The buildings are occupied by the soldiers and their families and it is currently the greatest place for babies in the world. We are very well treated by all officers, privates, men, women, children and even a dog called Sport took such a liking to us that he would bark and bite every Yankee that came in his way. The same dog stuck to us [as we traveled] to Johnson's Island, Ohio. But to our Fort we could pass from the inside of the fort up to the top of the parapets at each corner of the Fort. These passages are some 15 feet wide, covered over with arches. From the top of the fort we have the prettiest view of the surrounding waters in the world. New York harbor is in full view with all its shipping. The city of N. Y., Brooklyn, Hoboken, Jersey City, Long Island & Staten Island are all in full view of the fort. I can sit of a morning and can sing. All day [I can] see the vessels of all ports passing at all hours of the day. The U. S. flag waves in triumph over the fort inside. The whole lot is covered over with an entire shade of beautiful trees. Around the square is a beautiful walk of rock. There are large quantities of powder kept in the fort in a large place dug under the ground. The sally ports are guarded every night by sentinels. We have [as] nice [a] place for walking as can be desired and all in all I hope to be well satisfied as a prisoner can be, but it is horrible to be a prisoner.

June 4

Beautiful day today and I have had a fine walk with Col. Avery. I seen the graveyard where our poor dead prisoners are buried. Also, we have had a ball playing today with our Ga. and N. C. friends. We had some nice times on the ball ground. It made me think of my boyish days. Old Capt. McMullin, McMahan and Steegans all take a hand as if they were boys. We got the papers to read today. I am going to take prison life as easy as I can and I trust to pass it as pleasant as I can. I got me a law book today and if I am prisoner long enough I will see if I cannot be a lawyer, if it is a jack leg. Here comes the drums for dress parade—good night.

June 5

This day all the officers of the 28 Regt. went over to the castle to see to giving out clothes to our men, that we have got for them. I found Private Jenings[26] [Jennings] sick, from which he afterwards died.

June 6

Today we have all been interested in a yacht race that came off in the bay. It was opened by the firing of several cannon. We had a fine view from the top of the fort. I got G. B. McBride to come wait on us. I am now bearing down on my law book, but I think much of my lonely situation, of my brave boys that are now in the army undergoing all the hardships of life, [and of] my distressed friends. I hardly can bring my mind to bear upon anything. I today got a letter from Mr. C. C. Hardie, 47 Front St., N. Y., in which he told me he

---

[26]Private S. W. Jennings of Company I, 28th Regiment, died at David's Island, New York Harbor, June 28-30, 1862 of "fever." N. C. Troops, Vol. VIII, p. 214.

would furnish me with some clothing. I trust he will always be respected by all N. C. citizens, for he is very kind to her prisoners. If he was not to help them I do not know what they would do. Only think of my condition hundreds of miles from home, in a prison, a prisoner of war myself, without friends or acquaintances, or money, entirely cut off from communications or assistance, with only one suit of clothes and them on your back & been on there for four weeks without changing & all that time you have been exposed to all the rain & marching through mud & water knee deep for days at a time & sleeping on the cold wet ground with nothing under you. Then you have some faint idea of what condition I was in when I entered the fort. You also have some idea how bad off I was for friends that could help. About this time I applied to my Masonic[27] friends in the city of N. Y. I thought it a bold venture but a man drowning will do anything to save his life. In this, I was not disappointed, as one of the Masonic friends, a Dr. on the Island, called on me, examined me & told me I should be supplied all honor to the Ancient Fraternity. About this time, a never to be forgotten friend in Philadelphia, Pennsylvania, sent me a trunk of clothes & some money. O! how cheerful I now felt as I had some good clothes to put on & a little money to get me some little comforts with.

You can never know how to value such friends till you are a prisoner of war. My other companions, most of them, were as fortunate as myself & some more so. We all now begin to fix up & look like men again. Our living was miserable, the meat & bread was, not enough of it, badly cooked. [Our] Coffee [is] awful bad, but our mess got us some little chaffing dishes & then we cooked our own meat, bought us [some] eggs, butter & molasses & begun to live pretty well. But if we had got no money it would be bad. If you ever are a prisoner of war, I do hope you will have some money. The prisoners of Castle William came up six times a day, some of them into the fort to get their rations, but I was not allowed to talk with any of them or to go to the castle to see them. I

---

[27]Free Masons are members of a secret ancient fraternal order.

could go up on top of the Fort & see them come out to roll call or go down in some 200 yds. of them. This was very annoying to me but I must stand it anyhow.

June 15

Capt. G. B. Johnston had services in our room today. All our fellow officer prisoners came down to the services. We have some very pleasant times with our fellow officers. I frequently go to the reading of the <u>Dixie Discourser</u>, a small Rebel paper published in the Fort. The Editor is the distinguished high toned gentlemanly Rebel Capt. Sims of Fort Pulaski notoriety & from Savannah, Ga. He is a good writer & has some interesting communications to his paper. The paper is now in quite a flourishing condition & if we stay here long I think the <u>Discourser</u> will <u>Rebelise</u> the whole garrison. This is quite a treat to us to have the pleasure of reading a Rebel paper published by a Rebel in the Union Fort of the U. S., kept to incarcerate the rebel prisoners.

[The Commissary-General of Prisoners, Lieutenant Colonel Hoffman, issued the following orders for the prisoners to be moved on June 16th and 17th.]

OFFICE COMMISSARY-GENERAL OF PRISONERS
New York City, June 16, 1862.

Col. G. Loomis,
Commanding Fort Columbus, New York Harbor.

COLONEL: By direction of the Secretary of War you will please send to the depot near Sandusky in charge of a suitable guard all the rebel officers, prisoners of war, now in confinement at Fort Columbus. If possible so arrange it that they may arrive at Sandusky during the day as it would be difficult to cross to the island at night, and please inform the commanding officer of the time when they will arrive.

Very respectfully, your obedient servant,
W. HOFFMAN
Lieutenant Col. Eighth Infantry,
Commissary-General of Prisoners[28]

---

[28]<u>O.R.</u>, Series 2, Vol. 4, p. 28.

OFFICE COMMISSARY-GENERAL OF PRISONERS
New York, June 17, 1862.

Hon. E. M. Stanton
Secretary of War, Washington, D. C.

Sir: Pursuant to instructions heretofore received I have ordered that the rebel officers, prisoners of war at Fort Delaware and Fort Columbus, be sent to the depot at Sandusky, the movement to take place the latter part of the week unless an announcement of a general exchange of prisoners is made in the meantime when it would be unnecessary.

Governor's Island is better adapted for the reception of prisoners than any place in the interior and I would respectfully suggest that sheds for the accommodation of 5,000 be erected there immediately. The cost of transportation thence to an inland camp would go far toward covering the expense of the buildings. I would respectfully suggest also that bunks be put in Castle William for the accommodation of prisoners confined there. By this means more can be provided for there and good police and health will be promoted. Of course they would be so arranged as to be easily removed. I leave for Detroit this evening.

I am, very respectfully, your obedient servant,
W. HOFFMAN
Lieut. Col. Eighth Infantry,
Commissary-General of Prisoners[29]

[Diary entry continues]
June 18

Today we have notice of being moved to some unknown place we know not. We hope it is home but we fear it is not home. All is excitement in the prison about where we are to go. I do not like to be a prisoner, but as I am, I had rather stay here than go anywhere else. I can go to worse places

---

[29]O.R., Series 2, Vol. 4, pp. 35-36.

than this. Today the prisoners from Salisbury taken at Bull Run & other places came into the fort. They are a ragged set of fellows. They are encamped outside of the fort in tents. They are waiting to get their pay. They give a good acct. of their treatment in Salisbury, N. C.

The N. Y. ladies have come over to see the Secesh. If they were only Dixie Ladies how I would like & love to gaze upon them, but we are gazed at as if we were heathens but O! they cannot love like our Southern ladies nor make half such loving companions.

Fort Columbus, June 18/62

My Dear Father, Mother, Brothers & Aunt

I am quite well this beautiful day hoping you all are in the same health. I am somewhat discouraged as we are notified that we will be moved soon & rumor is that we go further north or into the interior of the country some 500-600 miles. I did hope to be paroled & come home as I am tired of war & its destruction.

I am glad that I can say that Federal officers & privates are very kind & courteous & Gentlemanly towards us all, for which I am glad of. Brother Vet, I want you to go to Raleigh or Goldsboro & draw my pay from the 28th of February to the first of July & so on, as my pay is due me which is every month. They owe me from Feb 28/62. Place my money somewhere where it will do me some good if I ever get home.

I give Dr. Bawm of our Regt $110 the morning after I was taken prisoner to send to you or father. He was Assistant Surgeon & taken prisoner, but was going to be sent home. I want you to write to Lieut. Ed Long, Richmond, Va. & find where Dr. Bawm [is] & his P. O. & initials of his name & write to him if Bawm is in camp to ask him to pay Ed my money, if [he] still has it & send it to you & for Ed to write to you where he is. I sent you a power of attorney to draw a receipt for me.

I will write as soon as I get to my destination. My men are all well. Give my respects to all my friends & may the good

Lord take care of you all as well as myself & if I never see you,
I hope to meet you all in a better world.

> Your son
>
> W. H. A. Speer, Capt.
>
> Co. I, 28th Regt. N. C. Troops

I hope the authorities will be so kind as to pass this letter.

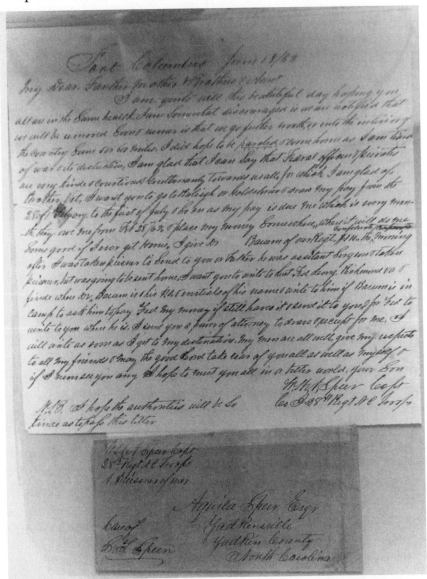

This letter was written when Asbury was a prisoner of war.

[Diary entry continues]

June 19

Today I received a uniform suit of clothes from Mr. C. C. Hardie & some other clothing, all of which will make me quite comfortable. I am under obligation to him and my Masonic friends as long as I live. He has the well wishes for his success & his families' by all the prisoners on Governor's Island. I feel now like I am as well fixed as any of the Yankee officers. The Yankee ladies are over again to get the last look at the Secesh. We are told this evening to where we go. We are to start in the morning at six o'clock for Johnson's Island near Sandusky, Ohio. I hate to go but I must obey. Some of us are now cast down & some of the Secesh officers have took a little too much of the ardent & are quite lively. The drums are beating for dress parade. So here we all go for the last time. Col. Loomis is commanding & here comes our tipsy Secesh officers all full of life & fun. I fear they will get into trouble. The dress parade is now over & back into the fort we go. All hands packing up now to be off in the morning—a lively time in the quarters. So to bed we go but some of our officers are quite noisy.

June 20

Capt. Clinton aroused us up early this morning. Early breakfast & off to the boat with our baggage we go. On the boat we march & off for Jersey City. As we leave the wharf, I see 4 ladies up to the left on the Island waving their hand-kerchief to our success. We bid farewell now to the old fort. I hope never to see it again under such circumstances. Although I have had, with my troubles & hardships, some pleasant times in the old fort. We are now at the Jersey side where the cars for Buffalo were waiting for us & here plenty of the Feds were to see the live Secesh & on the cars we get. After our baggage was seen safe on the cars, all our party occupied one car in charge of Capt. Clinton & Lieut. Miller. We came without any guard. As we passed some of the stations, the people—men, women, children & negroes—were there to see us. [At] some places there might have been 800 or 1,000 people to see us. It was amusing to see how foolish the people would act. When the car stopped, it was one general rush to the car doors & windows to see the live Rebs & then to hear their expressions. Some would say, "Well, Damn them, they are good looking men." "Damn such fellows, they ought to be hung, let's hang them." "By g.d., let's cut their throats. I kinder reckon they wish they were out of here." "Hello, what big rebels. They are good looking men." At one place, we stopped to get dinner & we had an excellent one. Here they got a good look at us all. Many of our officers were much admired for their gentleman[ly] appearance and manly soldier looks. We passed through much poor country but highly improved & portions of it very mountainous. The scenery was fine. I seen many things to engage my attention. [In] our party were very many [soldiers]. We got a fine supper on the road & arrived at Buffalo about 11 o'clock at night. Here we changed cars & started for Cleveland. We seen but few persons at Buffalo, as it was late at night. We got to Cleveland about good daylight, where we helped ourselves to a nice breakfast. From here we started for Sandusky—got there about 11 o'clock a.m. We marched from the cars straight for the boat, so quick no one hardly seen us. Upon the steamer we got, we crossed the lake (Erie) 3½ miles over to the Island where the barracks were to hold us. Maj. Pearson is in command here. This 21st day of June.

June 21

I never will forget outside of the barracks we were met by Maj. Pearson, halted & told we must give up all the money we had to him or be searched. This was quite humiliating. But as to myself, I only had $10, but I thought more of it than I would 500 in Dixie. But like men, we handed it all over. We were told by Maj. Pearson that we could draw on him at any time for what we would need. The sentinel opened the gate & we were marched into the prison. We were soon surrounded by hundreds of Secesh officers all anxious to see who we were & if they knew any of us. I did not know a man out of 1,300 prisoners now here. One man rushed up to me, slapped me on the shoulder & says, "I have found you at last. O, I ask your pardon," he says, "I thought you was my brother." He took me to his room with Lieut. Bohannon & give us our dinner. I felt badly, for we were now in a square lot of 16⅔ acres of land enclosed with a heavy slab of plank fence 15 feet high very strongly made. The top of the fence was filled with sharp spike nails, so you could not press the weight of your hands on them. On the outside of the plank fence is a platform all around the outside of the plank wall within 3½ ft. of the top. Upon this platform walks the sentinels who guard us. Out of this place we are not allowed to go, unless into the lake to bathe. There are 12 large block buildings in two rows on one side of the lot in which the prisoners are placed. We all have a bunk a piece to sleep in. I felt horrible at the idea of not being allowed to pass about as we did at Governor's Island, but still more at the tales told about the sentinels firing into our rooms. [They] had shot two men & wounding them severely "for life." This is dreadful to put them in prison & then shoot them like they were savages. We all messed ourselves off in messes. My mess mates were Maj. [Thomas] Lowe, Capts. Johnston & Stowe, Lieuts. Bohannon, Scott, Anderson & Wheeler. I was with a nice set of men. Our straw mattress & blankets come in & we are fixin' our bunks for sleeping & so we had a good night's sleep.

June 22

Today I got acquainted with many of the prisoners, among them I found an old cousin of mine [Dr. E. A. Speer][30] from Tenn., a Lieut. in the 18 Tenn. Regt. taken at Fort Donelson. A large portion of the prisoners here were taken at Donelson. I find upon the statement of men who know that we only had 250 killed & 7,110 taken prisoners & that the Yankees admit of a loss equal to all our killed & what they took prisoners of our men. The prisoners here are, the most of them, very respectable looking men from every state in the Confederacy. I have seen all the field officers here & I

---

[30]Dr. Ephraim Aquilla Speer (1838-1893) was Asbury's first cousin. Dr. Speer's father was Joshua Kennerly Speer II.

must say that, out of the large number, N. C. & Ga. has the two finest looking. C. M. Avery, Col. of N. C. & Col. Olmsted of Ga. are the finest looking officers here. I am perhaps partial to the above officers & perhaps to the N. C. & Ga. officers I have seen, & I know there is no more of gentlemen in the army than they are. And I must confess that while I am prisoner, that I am glad that I have been so fortunate as to have fallen among such clever gentlemen & officers. Various amusements are followed by the prisoners. The most are employed in ring making in which they use guts[?] & such[?] for the ring & put in it sets of gold & silver but mostly of shell of various colors, some of which are exceeding[ly] nice. The shells are obtained out of Lake Erie. We get them when we go into the lake bathing by diving after them. Many thousands of the rings, breastpins, shirt buttons, bracelets & watch fobs [short strap or chain attached to pocket watch] are made. Some of the prisoners pass their time making canes of peculiar stripe & kind, various pieces & kinds of furniture, and I believe the Southern men can beat the Yankees to death on inventions & tricks when necessity requires that they shall put their hands, mind, & wits to work. Other prisoners pass their time in playing at cards & various other games, while others are reading etc. So various men are engaged in various ways. I would like to get out of this place & look over the Island but, no Sir, I must stay here. When it rains we have the nastiest place in the world.

June 30

Today we got an extra this evening, giving us the exciting news of the commencement of the great battles before Richmond June 25. The news is gratifying & we have the greatest excitement ever I witnessed. Capt. Sims of Ga. is now on a stump reading the news. Around him are over 1,000 men, every now & then shouting & waving hats & slapping hands in wild enthusiasm. I never have seen as lively & noisy [a] time. We were informed by Maj. Pearson next morning that if we had another such demonstration in our bull pen that the guards will fire upon us. They have two block houses in which they have cannon loaded ready to fire into us at any time, also port holes for musketry. We are now duly notified that we are liable to be shot at any time. Think of this condition to be in, liable to be shot down at any time without any self defence. Had you not rather be somewhere else? Yes, I had rather be upon the battlefield every day than to be here in this miserable suspense and horrible condition of mind. Still the news we get today is better from Richmond. We hope now to soon be exchanged as we have got many of the Yankees prisoners. We have been visited today by a steamboat excursion from Sandusky loaded with men & women. [They] wave their handkerchiefs in derision of us. Our men are waving from their windows various looking flags. Some have black flags waving at the Yankees. These excursions come off every few days, but we have got to treating them with silent contempt. The Yankees now admit that they have lost over 50,000 men in killed & wounded & prisoners at Richmond—this is from their own papers.

Johnson's Island, Sandusky, Ohio
July 2, 1862

Dear Father & Mother

I write you a line today trusting it will find its way home & find you all well. I have written many letters to you all & trust some of them have reached you before this. I feel it my duty to write to you often hoping through the kindness of the officials they will let them pass. I have been sending them via New Bern, N. C. care of [Honorable] E. Stanly,[31] trusting he will pass them through.

I am very well, in as good health as I ever was. I could write you much but it will not pass as they have not time to read long letters. I do hope I will soon be released, either paroled or exchanged.

I have sent two or three powers of attorney to Vet to draw my money or pay. I hope some of them have reached him. I

---

[31]Edward Stanly, a Whig politician, became military governor of the occupied territory of North Carolina in May of 1862. A Lincoln appointee, Stanley resigned on January 15, 1863, because of his opposition to the Emancipation Proclamation.

William Sheppard Speer (1822-1915)
Sheppard Speer, Asbury's first cousin, was the son of Joshua Kennerly Speer II. Sheppard Speer was a writer, teacher, Campbellite preacher, abolitionist and diplomat during the Lincoln Administration. His brother, E. A. Speer, was a doctor in the Confederate army. His sister, America, married Asbury's brother Aaron. (Photo used by permission of Richard Speer, a great grandson of Sheppard Speer.)

want to dispose of it safely or invest it profitably. I have written how to apply it.

I am well treated by the Federal Officers, but I do feel badly being a prisoner of war. If I could hear from you all, but I suppose I never will till I get home. There are 1,119 officers here as prisoners. I find one of uncle JKS [Joshua Kennerly Speer] sons here—E. A. Speer—a Lieut.—he is quite a nice man. Sheppard Speer[32] is a minister to South America for the U.S. government. He was appointed a short time ago by the President.

We left 1,086 prisoners at Castle William, N. Y. City. S. M. Dozier and Evan Reece are there. We have reports here of a heavy battle before Richmond. Know not the result.

Write to me - a prisoner of war at Johnson's Island, Sandusky, Ohio, care of Maj. Pearson's Command. Give my love to Vet, Jimmy & Aunt.[33] My respects to all my friends. I think often of you all. Tell my dear Mother not to be or see any trouble about me. I will get home safe, I trust.

Your son,

W. H. A. Speer

I send this by way of New Bern, N. C. hoping that Wm. E. Stanly will forward.

[Diary entry continues]

July 6th

This is my birthday. Capt. G. B. Johnston has services for us today in our room. Today, I got some potatoes for dinner & we had a heavy rain storm. If it was not for the exciting news of exchange, I think this prison life would derange anyone. The excitement is certainly necessary for the life of a prisoner of war. Some of the prisoners tried to escape the other night [when] it was very dark. They, however, was discovered by the sentinel & was fired at by 2 sentinels, but no one was hit. They, however, came very near being killed &

---

[32]William Sheppard Speer (1822-1915), abolitionist brother of Dr. E. A. Speer, was a diplomat during the Lincoln Administration. His autobiographical memoir written in 1893 provides much information about the early history of the Speer family.

[33]Asbury's aunt, Nancy Speer, lived with her brother Aquilla until her death in 1882.

also quite near escaping. But what could the poor fellows do if they had got away, as the island is surrounded by a sheet of water over 3½ miles wide & very deep. Nothing would keep the prisoners in here if it was not that we are surrounded by water. Although some of us would be killed in attempting to escape but yet we would try it.

The horrors of the prison are so great I think I will never commit any crime to be put in jail, for if everybody could know & feel as I do, I think there would be no more jails built for any more offenders. We have the pleasure of the excursion boats coming over here with the women & men to look at us, but today caps all. The niggers are but today in two boats with their bands of music celebrating the day, August 1, as the birthday of colonization &, of course, they must come by & see the Secesh. O! how the black Bucks & wenches laugh at us.

Johnson Island near Sandusky, Ohio
July 18, 1862

Dear Father & Mother

I write you [a] line today trusting it will find you all well. I have no news to write to you. I am only tolerable well, having an attack of the rheumatism again. My health has been as good as it ever was, ever since I was taken prisoner until now. I think it was the affects of my taking off my flannel.

The weather here is very unsettled. I have seen some [of the] warm[est] days here as I ever seen in the South, but we have had cool days & nights for several days. I am very anxious to get paroled or exchanged. I want to come home, although I am as well treated as I could expect to be, but being a prisoner of war is as horrible a life as any man ever lived.

All the prisoners at Governor's Island, N. Y. have gone to Fort Delaware. I got a letter from the boys the other day. Old Man Jennings is dead. He was in my company. I have written to you or Vet every week ever since I was taken, but I fear the letters will never get to you. I have wrote to Vet to go and draw my money & sent him a power of attorney to do the same. If he has got any of them, I hope he has done so. If he has not & you get this letter before I get home, tell him to go to Richmond or Raleigh & draw it & do the best he can for me with the money. I have pay due me from the 28th of Feb. 1862.

I hope soon to be exchanged, as I think the governments will certainly agree upon some plan of exchange. May heaven bless you all & take care of us all till we all meet again. Write to me, as I do not know how long I will stay here. My love to all.

Your son,
W. H. A. Speer

[Diary entry continues]

August 2

Today two large steamboats [came] from Buffalo loaded with men & women all to see the bloody Secesh on Johnson's Island. Our spirits today are high on exchange. All hands are on the high horse tonight. There is plenty of grape in the prison this evening. Grape is the name we have for all the big tales that go around the prison. You can see the men from all parts of the prison now on the rush to crowd up at the sutler's [a civilian provisioner to an army post with a shop at the post] stand to hear what is the news. If it was not for the grape that comes into the prison, I hardly know how I could live. I do believe if Abraham keeps me in here much longer that I will become a lawyer as to asking questions & finding out the truth of all the reports.

August 4th

Today I finished my watch chain and I thought it was a very nice thing for me to make. I hope to live through this prison & the war & have my cane & rings that I have here made to show my great grandchildren. Capt. Farthing was taken to the hospital sick today. We have lots of grape in this evening—everybody is high up. All expect now to go home soon.

August 8

This evening, about 9½ o'clock p.m., there was one of our officers shot dead at his own quarters; just as he was going to his own bed. [He was shot] by one of the sentinels on the post. It was cold, willful and premeditated murder. The poor man told the sentinel that he was going to his quarters but yet the murderous sentinel fired & killed him. He was a young man, [a] very peaceable quiet fellow. His name was Gibbon & [he was] from Ark. It was one of the most horrible things I ever seen in life.

There was a strong effort for us all to make an attack on the sentinels, burst down the plank fence & take the guard's guns & try to secure the block houses & take the cannon, but to a man of good sense, it was an act of rashness to self destruction. If we had got out, how then would our case have been any better, for we then still would have been entirely surrounded by water. But good judgment & wise heads stopped us. The poor officer was neatly buried in a nice coffin & here is peace to his memory. There has [been] two other men shot in here before this, besides several shots fired into our quarters—only think of this treatment.

We have received the news of the battle of Cedar Mountain, Va. & the news is very good. High times in the prison now—one other victory for our cause.

August 14

Today, long faces in the prison exchange low down. We now begin to think that we will have to be hung certain.

Today, the 16th, is a day long to be remembered. Six Cols. & Lieut. Cols. are now very much excited, discussing the subject of being hung. They, however, do agree to draw lots with each other, [as to] which shall be hung first. It is right funny to see Cols. thus engaged & so anxious about their necks. I now do think that I may as well be looking out for signals. If the big fish are to be thus dealt with, what will little fellows like myself do. I think I will get off someway, for I am certain my neck was not made for the halter. I do intend to break out & try to swim the lake if I find there is a chance for me to be hung. We have many long faces through all the prison now, but tomorrow all will be up again, for the grape will come in some way & we foolish prisoners do believe & ever think as to exchange. Tomorrow has come & with it the grape has come to shore. We now hear that we are to leave here in a few days & everybody is high up. O, how happy we poor fellows now are.

August 23

This is the greatest day of all yet. We are all now being mustered for exchange. It would do you good to see us all now, heads all up & everybody is wide awake & all up for packing up immediately for Dixie, but I tell you all boys, you are in too high a way. You had better wait, for today 25,400 more poor prisoners have arrived from Camp Moten. They tell us bad tales about how our prisoners have been shot at the camp in cold blood. Many of the prisoners are political prisoners & I am sorry for many of them.

[According to Asbury's service record, he was sent to Vicksburg, Miss., on September 1, 1862. Three months passed before his next letter was mailed to his parents.]

Camp of the 28th N. C. Regt. 6 miles
from Fredericksburg on the R.R. Dec. 4, 1862

Dear Father & Mother

I got here last night with our Division. I have marched 280 miles from the 18th of Nov. From Winchester here it is 165 miles the way we have come & we were 12 days coming from there here. I have marched all the way & am quite tired. Otherwise I am well. I trust this will find you all well. I often think of all & trust that the good Lord will preserve our lives to all meet safe at the good old home. I have but little news to write you.

Our men have stood the march very well. They are as tough as hounds & as fat as bears but ragged. They are drawing plenty of pants, drawers, coats & shoes today, but they can't get any socks. All the people who can send their friends a [pair] ought to do so. Blankets are very scarce. We can see the Yankee fires & tents from this side of the River & there are a many one of them. Our whole army is in this section of the country, and is in a fine condition as to health & numbers. If there is a fight here it will be one of the worst of [the] war, as all the force is here & it will be a terrible affair. May I be protected if I am in it.

It is quite cold here. Two good snows on us but no rain as yet. If you get the chance, I want you to send me my old red striped blanket & Mother, I want [you] to sew my two old white blankets together & send them, as I need them to keep me warm of nights. I have all my baggage hauled now & I have nothing to do but go along. I am getting nothing to eat much. I want you to go buy me some cheese if you get the chance & some butter. I want to try to get a box of provisions from home if anybody comes & I want everything priced, as I am messing with Col. Lowe & Barringer[34] & will have to pay for them. I wrote to Vet to have me another pair of boots made & to get the leather from you & pay the money for all. My others were too small. Tell old Miss Hutchins that Isaac come to the company the other day and is quite well & has plenty of money. He has been at a hospital. All the men in the neighborhood in the company are well. Write when you can, direct to me by way of Richmond to A. P. Hill's Division. My love to all.

Your son,
W. H. A. Speer

[W. H. A. Speer wrote the following letter home after the Battle of Fredericksburg, Virginia. Because General McClellan was unable to deliver a knock-out punch at Antietam in September and was slow to follow Lee's retreating army, Lincoln relieved him of command on November 7, 1862, replacing him

---

[34]William Davidson Barringer, from Montgomery County, North Carolina, served as Captain in Company E of the 28th Regiment before being promoted to Lieutenant Colonel on November 1, 1862. N. C. Troops, Vol. VIII, p. 110.

with General Ambrose Burnside. Burnside attacked Lee at Fredericksburg on December 13, 1862, suffering a resounding defeat.[35]*]*

Camp the 28th N. C. Regt. Dec. 26/62

Ever Dear & Affectionate Mother:

I received your very kind & affectionate letter on yesterday & I wrote to you a few days before but I hasten to answer yours. It did me much good to get a letter from one who is as near to me & perhaps deeper in my affections than any person living. I have no news to write to you. We are doing the best we can living on beef & bread. We have had no Christmas. Yesterday was a very quiet day with us all. I do sympathize, dear Mother, with you all at home. The poor people are compelled to suffer & you & pappy are so tender hearted that I fear that you will divide till you will not have enough to do yourselves with. You must look out for yourself.

Dear Mother, let other people do the best they can, for you cannot support yourselves & everybody else. I know it is hard but we will have to do the best we can. I do want the war stopped as bad as anybody. I trust that something will turn up & stop the horror. The great battle the other day, Dear Mother, was as horrible as you can imagine, but thank God I came through safe & I do trust that I will be saved through all. I have full faith, my dear Mother, that I will not get killed & if I should I am confident that I will go to that good world where there are no wars to molest us. I put my trust in the good Lord & I believe he will take care of me. Tell Miss Hutchins that Isaac is gone to the hospital quite sick, but I think not dangerous. My love to Dear Old Pappy, trusting to see you all soon & the good Lord will preserve us all to see each other again.

I am your son,
W. H. A. Speer

---

[35]Boatner's Dictionary, pp. 310-313.

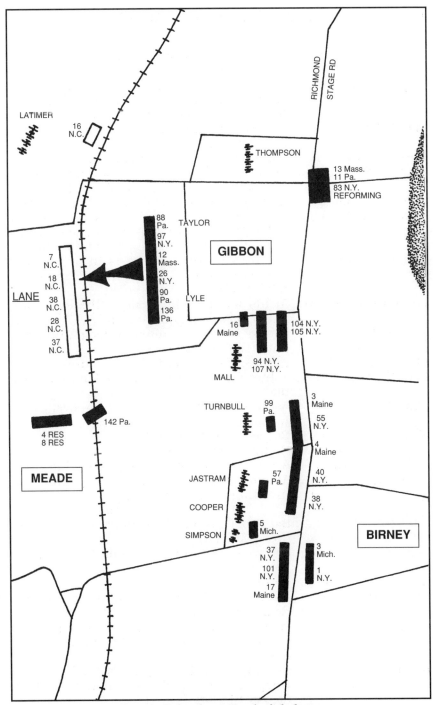

Lane's Brigade at Fredericksburg

Timeline 1863-1864

February 12, 1863....The shootout at the Quaker school (known as the Bond Affair) occurs.

February 20, 1863 ....Asbury is in winter quarters at Camp Gregg. He mentions the Bond Affair in his letter.

March 12, 1863 ....Asbury is promoted to Lieutenant Colonel.

March 13, 1863 ....Asbury's father tries to get him to resign from the army.

April 28, 1863 ....A tent revival is going on in camp.

May 7, 1863..............In his letter, Asbury gives a graphic description of the Battle of Chancellorsville.

July 10, 1863............Asbury describes the Battle of Gettysburg.

August 14, 1863 ......Asbury is camped near Orange Court House in Virginia. He mentions William Holden and the anti-war movement in North Carolina.

August 15, 1863 ......Asbury's brother James is in prison, but Asbury believes Chief Justice Pearson will release him.

February 18, 1864....In his letter, Asbury says "there is some national sin hanging over us..."

March 1864 ....Asbury is home on a month-long furlough.

May 5-6, 1864 ....Battle of the Wilderness

May 9-21, 1864 ....Battle of Spotsylvania Court House

May 12, 1864............Asbury has 113 men captured at Spotsylvania.

May 22, 1864............Asbury's regiment arrives at Hanover Junction.

May 22-26, 1864 ......Battle of North Anna River

June 1-3, 1864 ....Battle of Cold Harbor

June 18, 1864 ....Asbury's regiment arrives in Petersburg, Va.

June 22, 1864..........Asbury's regiment and Lane's Brigade capture 1,600 Union prisoners.

July 9, 1864..............Asbury is promoted to Colonel.

July 28, 1864............Battle of Gravel Hill. Asbury's regiment loses over 100 men.

July 29, 1864 ....Asbury writes North Carolina Governor Zeb Vance.

August 16, 1864 ......Battle of Fussell's Mill.

August 25, 1864 ......Asbury is mortally wonded at the Battle of Reams' Station.

August 28, 1864 ......Major Stowe, 28th N.C.T., writes a battle report describing the Battle of Reams' Station.

August 29, 1864 ......General Robert E. Lee praises North Carolina troops for their gallantry at the Battle of Reams' Station.

Battle Reports and Letters
1863-1864

Camp Gregg [Va.] Feb 20/63

Ever Dear & Affectionate Mother

I received your letter on yesterday and was truly glad to hear from you and that you are all well. I have but little news to write to you. We are in camp at the same place and have had some of the deepest snows I ever seen and plenty of rain. The roads are almost impassable. We have built a corduroy road from here to the depot to haul provisions on. It is said that the Yankees are gone off from the other side of the River. I hardly think it so, as we can see plenty of them on the other side & can see their camps from ours.

I suppose that Genl. Lee thinks there will be no fight here soon, as a very large part of our army has been going south for the last two weeks. Genl. Longstreet's command is, and has, all gone with many other troops. I fear that we will not have force enough here. Genl. Jackson is now in command of Northern Va. I trust that this war will stop before we have to do any more fighting but I am like you; I cannot see where it is to end. Many more I fear will yet have to be killed. If we can keep them from taking Charleston, Savannah, & Vicksburg then I am in hopes it will soon end but if they whip us there, it is very dark times.

Dear Mother, do not see trouble about me for I am trying to take as good care of myself as I can. I trust in the good Lord to save me in and out of battles & I know he will do it. I may get killed but [I] do not think I will. I believe the good Lord will preserve my life to come home to you again. I know you and my good Father are daily praying for me & I pray daily for myself to be a better man & to see you all.

I sympathize with you all in your troubles at home. I hope the poor people will yet be supplied with enough to eat. You must all keep enough for yourselves to live upon. I am glad Pappy has got a hand to help him. He gets very low. [I hope] he [James] is a good boy. Tell Pappy if he has not work on the farm, if he can get hides, he can make it pay him well to put him to work in the yard.[1]

O what a sad affair that was at the Quaker meeting house —poor men killed.[2] They all had better went to the army. They might have lived &, if killed, they would have died like men and not Tories. I am sorry that such things do exist, but some leaders in the county who told the men last summer if they would vote for them then [they] never should be enrolled & the law never should be enforced in the county are to blame for this. You said you was fearful that they would take Jimmy.[3] I have seen no law to take him yet but, if [they] do pass any such law, I want you to send him immediately to me & I will take care of him safe. I hope for you I can put him in a safe place. I hope you got the money for those things you sent me. I feel as thankful, dear Mother, as if I had got them. So give dear Father my love & you the same. May the Lord let us all meet again. God bless you all. Write when you can.

W. H. A. Speer

28th Reg. N. C.
Camp Gregg, March 13, 1863

Ever Dear and Affectionate Father

I write you a few lines in answer to your long and interesting letter Feb 28. I am ashamed at not writing sooner but I have had so much to do that I have not had the time, as I have and am now in command of the Regt., Col. Lowe having gone home on furlough.

I fully, my dear Father, realize the importance of your letter and feel the great weight of the truths in it, and I am fully aware of the great interest you and my dear old Mother take in my welfare, both in this world and in the world to come, and it is a thought that is on my mind daily, and I have

---

[1]Asbury's father, Aquilla Speer, was a tanner.
[2]Asbury is referring to the Bond Affair. See Appendix II.
[3]Asbury is referring to his brother James, who joined the local militia February 8, 1862. When the militia units disbanded in 1863, Home Guard units became part of the state military organization. Asbury's parents thought James would be drafted out of the Home Guard unit and placed in the Confederate army.

looked at it on all sides and have my mind fully made up to leave the service as soon as I can do it with safety to myself.

As to staying out of the army, I do not want to resign and go home and be forced to go into the ranks as a private. I would then give out immediately. If I resign now, and my resignation was to be accepted, there is an order of the Secretary of War now in force through all the army that as soon as an officer's resignation is received or an officer is dropped from the rolls for misconduct, if they are liable to any of the conscript acts, he is to immediately be enrolled and put in the ranks by the commanding officer of the Brigade. Now what is a man to do? He cannot resign without his Brigade command approving the paper. Then if it is received, it comes back to the Brigade commander before I know that the resignation has been received, and as he knows it first, he only has to enroll the resigned officer & notify him to go into ranks, and if he gets home he is there enrolled by the enrolling office, for a notice is to be sent to the county in which the officer lives to have him enrolled. I cannot lay out in the woods to keep out of the way of the enrolling officers. I have been trying to get some position where the conscript act would not reach me but I failed to do it safe.

I know that I am a little ambitious but not to heap upon myself worldly honors further than to do my duty as a man & anything short of that I would think dishonorable to myself and parents, but in trying to do my duty I do not think that I ought to endanger my health, for self preservation is the first law of nature. I know that my health is in a delicate condition and I have been feeling our Dr. as to a certificate of disability to resign upon, but he says that he cannot give me one yet and seems fully satisfied that there is no danger.

I never expect to arrive to any great distinction or renown by staying in the army, neither do I wish for the same, but the country is in a distracted condition. We are in the midst of troubles of every description and [it] does look to me that the wheels of government North and South have got off the track and everything is in the bad road to ruin. How it is to be stopped I cannot see, unless the great masses of the people

North & South resolve that this horrible war shall stop at all events, and shall not be allowed to exist any longer. For it looks as if the rulers have lost sight of peace to the country. I had rather be a good man and wise than to be in the place of Gen. Lee or any other man with all the worldly honors that can be heaped upon a man. I know that my enemies would like to know that I was killed or to hear of my death in any way, but I trust that Providence will not let them enjoy that pleasure while this war lasts. I will do all that I can to get out of the service as soon as I can and still more will I do to take good care of myself as I possibly can. I am in better health than I have been since I came back, but yet I am not as fleshy as I would like to be but I am of [the] opinion that it is because I do not have such things to eat as I like. If I was home, I would soon get fat again. I will, my dear Father and Mother, get out of the service as soon as I can stay out, and I cannot express to you the great respect and esteem I have for your opinions and judgment in these things.

I got my boots by Sam Harding.[4] They came in good time and fit me well. I would not take $100 for them. I have no camp news worth writing, only our men are very well. We have very hard living and rations short. The weather is quite cold. Perhaps the coldest weather we have had, we have today. I can hardly write. I am looking for my box every day when I will have something nice. I am sorry for the poor women of Yadkin and know that you have a hard time of it and much trouble with them. We have the triflingest congress in the world, or else they would do many things for the soldiers that they have not done, as well as many other things. I got a new lot of papers for James all fixed up this time so that there is no danger of their doing anything with him.[5] Gen. Lane is gone on furlough home & I got Col. Barbour,[6]

---

[4]Samuel Speer Harding, Asbury's cousin and brother of Greenberry Harding, served in Company I of the 28th Regiment. Harding and Speer were both killed at the Battle of Reams' Station in August 1864. Their bodies were brought back to Yadkin County, North Carolina, for burial.

[5]Evidently, Asbury arranged a legal deferment for James, which allowed him to remain in the Home Guard.

[6]William M. Barbour, a member of the "Western Carolina Stars" from Wilkes County, served as Captain in Company F of the 37th Regiment in James Henry Lane's Brigade. He was elected Colonel of the 37th Regiment on June 30, 1862. Colonel Barbour died at Petersburg, Virginia, on October 3, 1864. N. C. Troops, Vol. IX, p. 468.

who is in command of the Brigade, to approve all the papers officially, and I sent them to Vet by Isaac Reece, who started home on yesterday for furlough. Tell Jim if I get so I can't work, I shall charge him my support for keeping him out of the army. Tell him to get the papers from Vet. I will write again in a few days. My love to you and dear old Mother, also to James & Aunt. My kind regards to all the neighbors. Write when you can. May the good Lord spare us all to meet again is the wish of your

Son Asbury

Isaac Hutchins is well & all the neighborhood boys.

Camp Gregg, April 1, 1863

My Dear Father & Mother

I write to you a few lines today trusting they will find you all quite well. You must excuse me for not writing sooner, but I thought a few days ago we would move before this but have not as yet, but we are looking for it most any day. We have sent off all of our surplus baggage to Richmond and have nothing but what we can move with ease. I sent one of my blankets off & have three very large ones yet, which I can carry on my horse. I bought me another strong & fine horse the other day for $400. I sold the other one I had for what I give for him. He was a sorry horse but they are very scarce & high. I can sell the one I have now for $500.

I have no news. The Yankee army is now moving but we do not know where they intend to make an attack. They are in tremendous force I think. I was truly in hopes that something would turn up to stop the war but I now think the signs are dark and gloomy. It seems as if all the world & nations are holding their breath with their eyes closed & ears stopped to the awful shock of armies that is about to take place & no one to say quit. Who can foresee the end? All our authorities seem to have gone wild and the great American nation is ruined, but let us hope and pray for the better if the worst does come. I am more distressed for the poor women & children at home than any thing else. They will suffer, I fear, for something to keep life in existence.

The health of our army is pretty good & the men, poor fellows, are in fine spirits but exceedingly anxious for peace. Our men are bound to suffer much this season, as they cannot get anything hauled. All our wagon horses are very poor & many of them have died. It will be hard for us to move our artillery. The farmers ought to try & raise all the stock they can. We had a large snow on us March 30. It is now all gone & it is quite clear today but cool. We have no signs of spring in vegetation. The wheat looks like it would be no account. I fear that wheat will be a failure & what will be done. They have stopped furloughs & several are deserting from the army and I fear that it will get worse. I hope they will not take any more men from home for I think it will be starvation.

I am considerably improved in my health. My love of eatables has done much for me. You know that I have lived well till I came to the army and, when I come home, you know I get better immediately. I have been living well for the last month. I have plenty of potatoes & dry apples to do me two months. I am messing with James Barbour & he got a nice box from home. I do hope I will make some arrangement to get out of the army, for I am confident that rest will make me all right again. But I cannot get out, only by detail to attend to some government matter, for they now enroll every man who sends up his resignation before he can get out of camp and they are getting very strict on officers.

I will take as good care of myself as I can & keep from danger as long as I can and trust in the good Lord & pray to him for his protection and I believe he will. May he preserve our lives to meet again. God bless you all. My love to you & all the others. I was promoted to Lieut. Col. on the 11th of March.

Your son, W. H. A. Speer

Camp Gregg April 6, 1863

My Ever Dear & Affectionate Mother

I received your kind and affectionate letter the other day & was very glad to hear from you. It is always a great pleasure to me to get a letter from home & sometimes I think I write oftener than I ought to write, but I know the anxious feeling you all have for me and that is the reason I write so often & I feel it to be my duty to do so.

I have but little news to write you. We have just come in from picket—was out all day yesterday without any cover for our men and the snow was four inches deep and it was a very cold day. I got a house to stay in & a good fire to sit by, but our men had to take the weather. We have much bad weather this spring—snow, rain & mud. We do not have more than two or three clear days at a time. As soon as the weather clears off, & the ground gets dry, the Army will commence moving & then the fighting will commence, for neither Army can move much without a fight, for there is nothing between us but the River, unless one of the armies falls back & I think neither of them will do that without a fight.

I would be so glad if there would be no more fighting. I do not want to be in any more fights but if I have to be, the good Lord has preserved me through many dangers & in him I put my trust. [I] pray for my protection & I do believe he will [do so]. I know that I have a Christian Father, Mother, Aunt and many friends who are praying for me & if they only have faith, their prayers will be answered. But while I pray to the Lord to preserve my life & protect me, I pray for his holy spirit to help me to be & live to be a better man and, let me live long or short, [I] intend to try to live like a Christian man & die happy & go where my dear brother & sisters are.

I fear there will be much distress & trouble at home & in the entire country. With the poor class of people, it looks like trouble is only about to begin. I have no idea what is to become of the country if the prayers of the Christians do not prevail. I fear that we are lost. I am sorry that Pappy has the tooth ache, so he ought to have it pulled out. I sent Vet an order for my bed & bed clothes at Dr. Benham's, also for another bed & clothes I had at Mr. Isaac Hutchins. He wrote to me he had got them, so he can keep them. I have two large trunks & box[es] full of books at Dr. Benham's [that], if I was to never get home, you must get. Vet wrote to me he needed the beds.

Tell Aunt I want to see her & would take much pleasure in answering her questions. I hope her dreams will be true. I am going to Richmond in the morning on business for the officers. I got a furlough for four days. I would have been mighty glad to have come home, but I could not get off. I hope to be able to come home soon. My health is much improved. My box was a great thing for me. I am under many obligations to you for it. Tell Father that I have been living on shad for four days & have five nice ones salted up—how I wish he had them. Our men ketch [catch] hundreds of them here in the River. Tell Jimmy if he had not [does not have] my bridle made, he need not, as I can make out. I will write to him in a few days. My love to you, Father, Aunt, Jimmy, & kind regards to all of my friends & neighbors. May the good Lord bless & take care of us all is the desire of your son.

W. H. A. Speer

Camp Gregg April 28/63

My Ever Dear Father & Mother

I write you a few lines today trusting they may find you all enjoying all the blessings of an ever kind Providence. Dear Father, I received your kind letter of the 19th. I was, as I always am, glad to hear from those who I hold most dear on earth. I am glad you had that old tooth pulled, for you will not suffer so now. I am sorry to hear that my dear Mother is unwell. I hope she is by this time well. I would feel as if I was lost to lose my Mother. I hope you all will have enough of provisions to do the poor women & children of the soldiers. If they cannot buy it, I am for their going to those who have it horded up for high prices & taking what they want, for it is no time to hord up the substantials of life, [having] only enough to do their own families. It is hoped that enough will be provided for all. I expect we will have a hard time of it in way of eatables. Our enemies now expect to starve us out, but if the men, women, & children will do their duty at home, I hope there is no danger. I trust we will have to call for no more men from home. I see from the Yankee papers that they are preparing to recruit their army only by enlistments & that

I think will fail. 300,000 of their men's time is out in a few days & they say that unless they meet with some early success that there will be but little fighting this summer. I hope this may be the case, but if they do not advance, I am certain our army will, for I do not think that two large armies can lay so close together this summer.

It is to be regretted that our currency is depreciating, for without a currency we cannot do much if we are not successful I think.[7] One currency is as good as another, for it will all go down alike. I believe I would let my leather lay, for it is a certain investment. If I possibly could get them worked in, I would get all the hides I could & work them in. If you get them far enough along, they will not damage. You can then finish tanning & have them worked out when you please.

We have a revival going on in our Regt. & it is general through the army. Our Chaplain is doing much good. We have 290 members of the church in our Regt. as joined yesterday. I hope it will go on till all of the men & officers become Christians. If we were not right in the outset in this war, I do think that the great outrages, crimes & wicked conduct of our enemies has put us in the right. If the people at home will do their duty & act right & the men in the army do the same way, the good Lord & God of battles is & will be on our side & what can withstand our armies.

I am as well as common. I now hear heavy cannonading going on up the River, & if there is fighting to be done, we may expect it soon. My love to you all & respects to all the neighbors. Write, Father, whenever you get the chance, as I have no right to complain about letters. May the good Lord preserve our lives to meet at home again in peace. As ever, your affectionate son,

Asbury

P.S. Tell Aunt I have got one of the apples she sent me yet & I have plenty of dried fruit. Tell Capt. Thad Reece to send me the date of his brother's death & when he was last paid so

---

[7]Because of the large amount of paper money in circulation, the South experienced runaway inflation. According to James McPherson, "the South's unbalanced agrarian economy simply could not produce both guns and butter without shortages and inflation."

Capt. Bohannon can make out the proper inventory of his effects & what is due him. Capt. [Neal] Bohannon & Lieut. Si [Bohannon] & Snow, with many of the men, send you their kind regards. Excuse haste.

[*After Burnside's defeat at Fredericksburg, Fighting Joe Hooker assumed command of the Army of the Potomac. Hooker seized the initiative at Chancellorsville and, at first, outmaneuvered Lee. But Hooker hesitated, which allowed Stonewall Jackson to make a 14-mile march around the Union army, attacking its exposed flank. Chancellorsville came to be known as Lee's masterpiece.[8]*]

Camp Gregg May 7, 1863

My Ever Dear Father and Mother

Thank the Good Lord and bless His holy name I am well and safe and sound from one of the most terrific fights (perhaps for the numbers) that the world ever witnessed. I never shall be able to thank and praise His excellent name enough for His protecting power over me.

We left this camp 9 days ago today. We went to Fredericksburg that day and formed line of battle. We stayed there till Friday morning till day break (but did no fighting but was under the shells of the enemy Thursday) at which time we took up march for Chancellorsville. We were under the fire of the enemy all day Friday and fighting also Friday night. Saturday morning we left by day under Gen. Jackson and went around the enemy's flank, traveling 20 miles. Attacked them in their rear about two hours by sun and drove them four miles by dark—we continued to fight till 3 o'clock Sunday morning. We had a hard fight for two hours Saturday night from 1 o'clock till 3, where I got slightly wounded on the knee, which kept me out of the fight Sunday, but I reported for duty Monday.

But Sunday was the bloodiest day of this war! We had 40,000 men engaged and the enemy 120,000 nearly all day.

---

[8]Boatner's Dictionary, pp. 136-139.

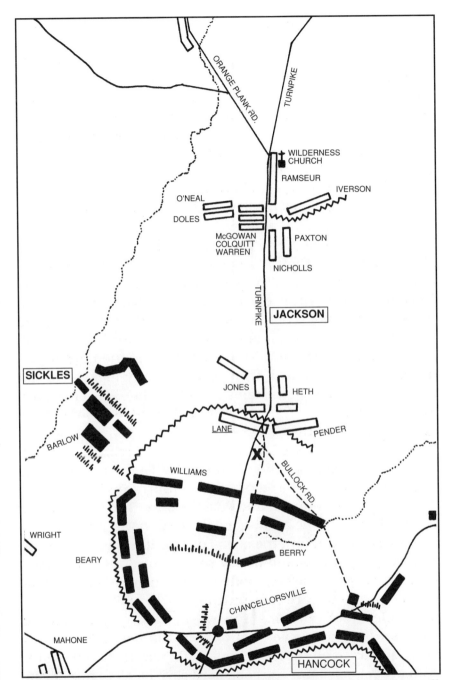

Lane's Brigade was spearheading the night attack when Stonewall Jackson was shot at the Battle of Chancellorsville — X marks the approximate location.

As I was not in the fight from my wound, I was a spectator on my horse. O Father, the scene was awful. I cannot describe it to you as it was and will not try. Our men charged a battery of 28 pieces of cannon ½ miles 3 times before it was taken and it was charged many times by other Divisions, but our men at last drove them off at a great loss of life. Monday there was but little fighting done and also Tuesday and Wednesday, except picket fighting all the time and artillery. Tuesday night the Yankees crossed the River and we came here today—during all this time they were fighting from Fredericksburg to Chancellorsville—a distance of 14 miles, but we have drove them at all points.

Our loss in killed and wounded foots up about 10,000. The enemies, for their statements, over 20,000 killed and wounded. We have over 10,000 of their men prisoners. I visited a part of the battlefield, and O, the destruction of life and property. I will not give the names of the killed and wounded as you will soon see them in the papers. My old company lost no man as we know killed nor none of the boys in the neighborhood wounded. Our Regt. was very lucky—we lost no officer in the field killed or any of the line officers. A few wounded, we lost 17 killed and 85 wounded. Some of the Regts. lost half of their officers and men.

There was a Yankee hospital caught on fire and burnt up some 500 of their wounded and 10 or 15 of ours, and the woods caught on fire from shells and burnt up hundreds of their dead and wounded and some of ours. Too bad to think of, but they are gone and I hope they will never return.

I am well and thank the good Lord for it. I want to see you all very badly and would nearly give my life for the privilege. I hope I will get off before another fight. I hope you have a fine spring—the trees are just putting out here. Tell Jimmy to plant plenty of potatoes and raise some sugar cane for molasses. My love to you both and to Jimmy and Aunt. My kind regards to all the neighbors. Tell them their sons in the 28th are yet safe. May the good Lord save us all to meet again is the wish and prayer of your affectionate son.

W. H. A. Speer

Camp Gregg May 19, 1863

Ever Dear and Affectionate Mother.

I write you a line today trusting it will find you all quite well. I have no news to interest you. We have been very quiet ever since the great battles. Our men have been terribly broke down from the trip and many of them are very sick. We have had as high as 175 sick per day, but it is not so bad now as it was. The men have had flu & diarrhea, & I do not wonder at it or if they had all died, for we were marching all the time & fighting for 9 days &, two of them, the nights was rainy & muddy as you ever seen. [For] 3 days the men got nothing to eat & it was awful. We fought the Yankees 150,000 with 40,000 men.

I have been very sick ever since the fight. A part of last week I was sicker than I have been since I was at home last spring. I am quite poor & feeble now, but much better than I have been. As I am now improving, I suspect to be well soon. I have been so I could not eat, but I sent off some miles & got me butter at $3.00 per lb. & some eggs at $1 per doz. & have been getting sweet milk at $1 per gal, so I am sorter [sort of] doing. I have never reported on the sick list yet, although many field officers in the Regt. is now sick & I have had everything to do. [However] Major Stowe is now ready for duty, so I can be relieved. But, Mother, do not now see lots of trouble about me, for I am much better & will soon be all right. I feel so thankful to the good Lord for answering our prayers in saving my life through that awful battle. My wound lamed me for some time, but I only stayed away from my Regt. one day for it.

Dear Mother, I thought I would tell you & dear Father I joined the Church some months ago here in camp. I felt it to be my duty & thought it right to do so. I trust the good Lord will, by his mercy, help me to live as I ought to do. Our revival is still going on & I hope all will be truly converted. The good Lord will, I believe, spare me to come home, but if I fall I am confident all will be well with me.

I want to see you all very much & hope I can get a furlough soon to come home. I can't give any news as to what the Yankees are doing. There are some of them in sight yet. I hope that your crops look fine & everybody is hard at work. The boys from the neighborhood are all well. Give my love to my dear Father, Aunt & Jimmy. I wrote to him a few days ago. My kind regards to all the neighborhood & friends. I will write in a few days again. Some of you write when you can. May the good Lord preserve us all to meet again is the prayer of your son.

W. H. A. Speer

Camp Gregg May 22/63

Ever Dear Father.

I have been looking for a letter from some of you for several days, but Jimmy's was the last one I got. I fear some of you are not well or I would have got a letter before this. I have no news to write to you.

Many of our men are yet quite sick with the bowel complaint—at least ⅓ of them—and if we have to make a forward movement there will be ¼ of the men for duty now that will give out. I never have known men so prostrated in my life from 9 days of labor but [it] goes to show to what extent the men were exposed. There is, however, a camp rumor that we would make a forward movement. How true, I am not able to say, but I hardly think it so, for I cannot see how we can support our army on the other side of the Rappahannock, as we have no R.R. There are a great many troops gathering in this section of the country and Lee may move over the River.

Father, the future looks dark & gloomy. No man, I think, can see the end with any satisfaction. If we can hold out at Vicksburg, the gloom will not be so dark, but if we lose Vicksburg it is a great blow to the C.S.; I think it of more importance to us than Richmond, but we have but one place to trust for the success of our cause and that is in the good Lord.[9]

---

[9] By saying Vicksburg is more important than Richmond, Asbury reveals his expertise as a strategic thinker. Lee, along with the high command in Richmond, was debating this very issue on May 16. As we know, the decision to invade the North, instead of protecting the South, led to the Battle of Gettysburg.

If our cause is a just one & we do right & trust in Him as we should it is of little difference how many Yankees are against us. But if not, we must sooner or later fall, for our enemies out number us 3 or 4 to 1 and [are] greatly our superiors in arms & equipments, & fight nearly as well. I am perfectly resigned to my fate, for I believe the good Lord will take [care] of me & I will get home safe. If I fall, I will fall prepared for death, if it is my lot to leave the world in that way. But I have the strongest hopes of a different state of things as to my case. The Lord will provide for those who put their trust in Him.

I am quite unwell at this time & have been for the last two weeks or ever since the fight. I am very poor & shaky. I look as poor as you ever seen me since [I was sick] last March a year ago. I have, however, improved some & am better. I tried to get a sick furlough but cannot. If I cannot do that soon, & I do not get any better, I intend to make an effort to resign. There seems to be nothing the matter with me except perfect weakness & [dis]ability. I truly hope that none of my Brothers or relations will ever have to go through what I have.

I hope you are all having a fine spring & summer for gardening & crops. I hope you have a good garden of potato patches. [Hope] Mother has plenty of beans planted & onions & cucumbers. I hope I will be home to help eat them. I understand crops look finely everywhere. I hope the good Lord will bless us with good crops.

Capt. Bohannon is getting better. All the boys about the neighborhood are well. James Reece's son is a mighty good boy & soldier. Dan Hall not much account. Isaac Hutchins is quite well. Tell James Davis to write to David Cockerham. He is a good soldier & looks lonely, for Reece nor Davis either writes to him. He frequently talks about them & his children. I hope you are getting on well with your work & my advice to you is to do the best you can. Let things get as hard as they may, every man's duty is to himself first & then to his fellow man. Give my kind regards to all the neighbors. My love to you and Mother, Aunt & Jimmy. I hope to live to meet you all again at home. I will write in a few days. May the good Lord bless us all is my prayer.

Your son,
W. H. A. Speer

I just got a letter from Vet—sorry to hear that Mother was sick. Hope she is well. [I] was glad to hear that you was all doing as well as you could. This is the 4th letter I have written to you, Mother & James since the battle. I will write in a day or two.

Camp Gregg May 27 1863

Dear Father & Mother,

I drop you a few lines today trusting they may find you well. I have received no letter yet from any of you since James wrote the 1st of the month. I am confident you have written, but I have, by some means, not got them. I am almost frantic to hear from home. I trust that you have received mine, for I have written every week, sometimes oftener.

I have no news. Our men are, many of them, on the sick list yet. Sickness is more prevalent than I ever knew it before. Several of the bad cases are going off to the hospitals. None of the men [from] around Yadkin are sick as yet, except David Cockerham. He has been gone to the hospital some time.

The weather is quite warm. Until the last few days it has been cool. Today is my birthday in the way of battles. This is the day, 12 mos. [months] ago, we fought the battle of Hanover C. H. and the Yankees got me. I do not think they will get me today. I trust that they will never get me anymore.

Dear Father, things look very gloomy to me, although the army is a better place for a man to keep in good spirits than at home, but when I look to the future, all looks dark. I can see no signs of an early peace, though it may come in a few days. God, send it soon. But on all sides, battle seems to be the order of the day. The enemy is over the River in full view of us and are making some demonstrations. If they cross over we will have a desperate time of it, for we have a strong force here now to what we had before. Two Brigades of N. C. soldiers have come up here & they are very large. Poor old N.

C. men. It seems they have to get it in all the fights. There are great responsibilities [hanging] over those who brought on this war.

We are having considerable religious excitement in all our army and there seems to be a prospect of much being done in the good cause. I have been writing to you that my health was not good & that I was quite feeble. I have improved some and feel much better than I did 15 days ago and hope I will soon be as good as common. If my health does not get much better, I will do my best to resign on surgeon's certificate, if I can get one from the Drs. It is very hard for a man to get out of the army. If I had a detail to go to some place out of active service, I could do better. Give my kind regards to all the neighbors. I hope you are all getting on well & have a nice time for work. My love to you both & James & Aunt, and may the good Lord bless and preserve us all & let us meet again at home.

Your son
W. H. A. Speer

I have got no letter from Vet lately.

[Gettysburg]

MD, Haggerstown, July 10, 1863

Dear Father, Mother, Brothers and Aunt:

Through the goodness of the blessed Master I am alive and well. But when I look back and see what I have just come through by His protection, I am unable to thank Him as I ought for the wonderful goodness exercised over me. Dear Father, the tale is too awful to be told.

Our grand army made its way into Pa. across the Blue Ridge to Gettysburg PA where we met the enemy on the 1st of July and had a battle on the 2nd and 3rd—the most terrific battles the world ever seen or human beings even engaged in. I will now try to describe it to you. On the 2nd and 3rd days of July there were 275 pieces of cannon engaged on our side and over 500 on the Yankee. I know we had 275 pieces and their prisoners say that they had 500 in action. You can't form any idea of the scene. Added to the engagement was

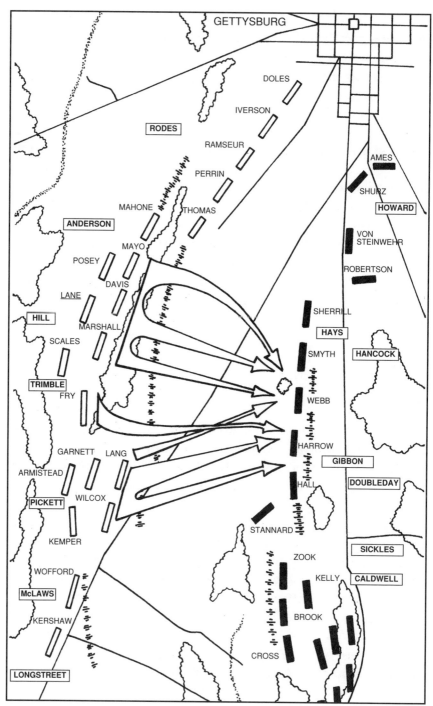

Pickett's Charge at Gettysburg

some 80 or 100,000 infantry. I was with our Regt. and Brigade in it all. I went into the fight on the 3rd with 326 men with guns and could only muster next day 100 men. After some of the slight wounded coming back and two or three stragglers, I have 118 men in the Regt—the balance are killed, wounded or missing. There was only 12 men killed dead that we know of, but we have 95 men that cannot be accounted for who was either killed or wounded or left inside of Yankee lines, as we made a charge to take their strong-hold and could not hold their position but had to fall back and left our wounded and killed on that part of the ground in the hands of the enemy.[10]

The charge was almost the last hope as the heights had been stormed on both ends by a flank movement and could not be held, and then we had to storm it in front, and had to fall back. The 3 days of July will be long remembered by the people of N. C., as the N. C. Troops did nearly all the fighting that day and have nearly been destroyed—none of the Regts. in our Brigade are as large as a good full company [125 men]. Pender's old Brigade has but about 90 men for duty. Those large N. C. Regts. just came to this army—some of them 1,200 strong—only can muster 2 and 300 men, but our Division and Corps suffered worse than any other by much. If all others were as we are we would hardly have any army.

I have sent on a list of the casualties in the 28th which you will see soon. In my old company, Jones Holcomb, Jinas [Jonas?] MaCokey were killed dead. A shell exploded in the line as we were charging, killing them both dead, wounding 3 others and knocking me down. Sgt. Cast and Buchanan sup-posed killed, Sgt. Hendricks wounded through the legs and in the hands of the enemy. John G. Holcomb—thigh and hand, left at our hospital in the Yankee hands. J. G. Danner mortal, since dead. E. H. Reece severe and [we] left D. C. Hall. ___ is across the lines. J. G. Reynolds in the Yankee lines wounded. Sgt. S. Bohanon slight, H. H. Snow severe. M.

---

[10]Asbury is referring to Pickett's Charge.

Greenberry Patterson Harding (1842-1932)
Asbury's cousin Greenberry Harding was the brother of Samuel Speer Harding, who was killed at the Battle of Reams' Station. According to his grandsons Felix and Harvey Harding, Greenberry was hit five times at Gettysburg. He was also wounded at Gaines Mill, Fredericksburg and Gravel Hill. He lived to be 90 and, when he died, was buried with a minnie ball in his shoulder. (Photo used by permission of Frances Harding Casstevens and Felix Harding.)

Harvey Harding (left) holds a picture of his grandfather. Felix Harding (right) holds his grandfather's pistol. Felix still remembers many Civil War stories that his grandfather told him.

Carter severe, N. C. Dozier slight. Berry [Greenberry] Harding[11] struck 3 times slight. C. V. Hutchens, S. N. Johnson, both slight. All these are inside of our own lines. Capt. Apperson took in 24 men and only came [out] with 4 unhurt. Col. Lowe out, Marler in the Yankee hands. Capt. Lovell's company—every man in it was struck. Lovell wounded severe—S. T. Thompson wound[ed] very severely. As I took in 38 officers, I came out with only 17. We took into the fight 38 officers and have only 16 for duty. So, you see that we have suffered terribly on all sides. We charged a battery one mile off and pass[ed] over a very level piece of ground all the way with 70 pieces of cannon throwing all sorts of missiles into our ranks. We had two columns cut down and destroyed. I will close this horrible picture for you to finish.

Written from on the battlefield at Hagerstown, July 13, 1863

I finish my few hurried lines. We have been in line of battle for 3 days now. Skirmishing all yesterday and the day before, and it is now going on with some artillery firing often at that. We have our entire army entrenched and the enemy is in full view, and we are expecting an attack every moment—if they attack us here, if I am not mistaken, they will get what no army has got before. I received your letter of the 23rd and Father's of the 30th—was so glad to hear from all—O, how I want to see you all. I hope there will be no fight as I am confident we will cross the River. We are out of rations—some of our men have not had bread in 48 hours. Our foraging in the country is cut off, and we cannot get any from the other side of the River and drought will compel us to cross over. Our Army is in good spirits and confident of victory.

Camp Near Orange C. H. August 14/63

Dear Father & Mother

This beautiful morn I drop you a line trusting it may find

---

[11]Greenberry Harding, brother of Samuel Speer Harding and a cousin of Asbury Speer, was, according to his grandsons Felix and Harvey Harding, hit five times at Gettysburg. Felix says he remembers a story that Greenberry told him about wagons going over the battlefield and picking up the dead. Greenberry was lying there wounded and when they came to him they said, "Here's a live one," and they did not put him on the wagon with the dead soldiers. Greenberry also received wounds at Gaines Mill, Fredericksburg, and Gravel Hill. He went to his grave with a minnie ball in his shoulder. N. C. Troops, Vol. VIII, p. 212.

you all in the enjoyment of all that can be realized in these times of war & distress. We are here still in our camp in a beautiful place. We have been here for 12 days. Our men are in lively spirits as ever I seen them. They seem to have forgotten all their former hardships. They are getting plenty of rations. [They] all got new clothes & newly shoes & have just been all paid off up to the 30th of June, and the prospect is that we may stay here some time, unless the enemy advances on us, which I think is not likely, as he is too much crippled to advance & they have sent home many of their men and officers to get conscripts. Many of their men's time is out. From their papers, it seems that they are having difficulties to overcome as great or greater than we have. I think they are as tired of the war as we are, but fanaticism will drive on the war I fear. I see but little signs of peace.

If we had not gone into P.N. [Pennsylvania], I think it would have been better for us, although I believe that the battle of Gettysburg has done more to strike terror to them than anything else. There is much excitement among the N. C. Troops about the peace talk at home & the course of the N. C. Standard[12] meetings have been held in all Regts. & a convention held at Orange the 12th passed many resolutions denouncing an unconditional peace or a surrender. I was not in the meeting. I think they will amount to but little.

I am sorry that so many deserters are at home & so many in our county. I do hope the people will try & get them all to come back under Jeff Davis' proclamation & do their duty. Capt. Clark of this Regt. is detailed to come home after deserters & those who are liable to conscription. If he comes to Yadkin, I hope he will call and see you. He is a nice man, a Christian man, unassuming. I do hope the people will look at things as they are. If the deserters do not come back, our county and country will be flooded with our own troops and the Fathers, Mothers, Wives & Relatives of the deserters will

---

[12]During the summer of 1863, William Holden, editor of the Raleigh <u>North Carolina Standard</u>, organized anti-war meetings across the state that, in the minds of many Confederates, were acts of treachery.

William Woods Holden, editor of the Raleigh <u>North Car-olina Standard</u>, was a leader of the peace movement in North Carolina. He was defeated by Zeb Vance in the 1864 election for governor. (Photo used by permission of Department of Cultural Resources, N. C. Division of Archives and History, Raleigh.)

all be brought off to Richmond—the women put into the factories and the men in the army & fortifications, let them be old or young. Will not this be dreadful? If the deserters do not come back [and] we all know that their friends are feeding them, & if they cannot be got, their friends will be taken in their sted, & the war will be brought home and God forbid that it may ever get to our county. But it is fast coming.

The people will not believe it, but I have told them things years ago that trouble was coming & they did not believe it; but it came & so will this. I want to see peace as bad as any man & I am as sick or sicker of the war than any man, but backing down will not do now. It would have done some time ago but [it] is too late now. A strong front will do us more good than anything else. If the absentees were here, our army would be large enough to drive the enemy out of Va. at once. I do trust the war will soon close without another battle. Mother, I want you to have me two shirts made if you can. I want them colored so they will not show dirt & I don't care how strong they are. My old calicos is about to give out. I have had them over a year.

If there was any field officer here but myself, I could now get to come home, but there is no one but myself here to command. I am coming home first chance and I would like to come to stay. I am living pretty well. I get potatoes to eat sometimes & green apples to fry—no beans. I made me a few pickles the other day. They eat pretty well. I would love some beans & Mother's pickles. O, how good the peaches & apples are & watermelons. Tell James to save some as long as he can. Maybe I can get home before they spoil.

I want Father, Vet, & James not to take any part in these county meetings of no sort. Let them do it all themselves & you all will not be to blame in anything. I am determined to get out of the war first chance, if the good Lord spares my life. I got a letter from Vet dated 5th of August, but O it was so gloomy a letter. My love to you all. May the good Lord spare all of us to meet at home.

Your son, Asbury

Isaac Hutchins is well.

Dear Father

I received your kind & affectionate letter of the 8th yes-terday after I had written the within and it is useless for me to attempt to describe to you my appreciation of your let-ters, for I have not the language to express it. They are always full of expressions of affection, which is felt by me better than I can express it. The great affection I have for my dear par-ents is beyond my describing. I can only make it known by my conduct as a man & respecting and honoring them by my acts. I feel that one of the great debts that I owe my protec-tor is the blessing of such kind, affectionate and Christian parents.

You speak of the gloominess of your letters. It is a gloomy time & all feel sad at the condition of things and the prospects before us. I feel the condition of things as much as any one & I am for hostilities stopping to see if there can-not be someway found for a settlement. But at this stage of things, I am opposed to a back down on our part without the North doing the same for various reasons, which I have not the time to write. As to peace propositions from us, that would all be correct. It would put us on the side of human-ity. Vice President Stevens started for that purpose but was stopped at Fortress Monroe. I sometimes think the fighting is over with. It may be because I want it ended so. I do not won-der at the Secessionist being alarmed. They are the cause of the war. I do not believe that God had any more hand in bringing on the war than the child unborn did. The seces-sionists are the men to blame & if the people punish any one at home, I hope they will be the first to ketch it. Men who, when danger stares them in the face, back down from what they did & said are not fit to be called cowards. They will get what is due them some of these times. I trust they will not take James off. I don't think they can. If they do, I want him to come to me. You & Vet can get Vance[13] to send him to me by going & seeing him, but they cannot take him. Did you get

---

[13]Asbury is referring to North Carolina's Governor Zebulon Vance.

the letter with the decisions of the courts I sent you? You need not send me the Isaac Hutchins receipt—I paid him $50 at Kinston, as for receipt enclosed. Pearson[14] will release James I am certain. I may be mistaken, but I think I am right.

Sept 13/[1863] Camp near Orange C.H.

My Dear Father,

I write you a few broken lines tonight, truly hoping they may find you all well. I received your kind letter last evening by Dozier and was glad to hear from you all, although your letter was a gloomy one. It cannot be otherwise if a man writes the truth these days.

I am so sorry for you and my dear old Mother and truly do pity Jimmy for being so very unfortunate.[15] I must confess that with all my bouyant spirit I do feel depressed when I look where I stand & what I have gone through with and nothing apparently yet accomplished. But nearly all of my countrymen [are] on the other side of the question. It is enough to cower the stoutest heart a man can profess. And this, too, may be the last time I may ever write to you. For we have been hearing that awful boom of cannon this evening at Culpepper & the report is, by the men from there, that the Yankees hold the place. Some of our wounded have already come on the down train and I have orders to hold my Regt. ready to move at any time. I trust it is only a cavalry raid.

I trust the good Lord will preserve my life. I have always believed He will preserve my life. If it was not for the confidence I have in Him, I don't know how I [would] ever go into battle. But I may fall. My time may come and I may be a victim to the demand of this cruel war. If I fall, I trust to meet my dear Brother and Sisters before us gone, with all you I leave behind. If I can reach that heavenly world above, I will be free

---

[14]As Chief Justice of the North Carolina Supreme Court, Richmond Pearson was a thorn in the side of the Confederacy. Having little sympathy for the Confederate cause, Pearson repeatedly held the Conscription Act to be unconstitutional. When conscripts appealed their cases to Judge Pearson, as did Asbury's brother James, Pearson turned them loose.

[15]James Speer's parents, Aquilla and Elizabeth, were afraid that even Judge Pearson would be unable to prevent him from serving in the Confederate army.

from all the toils and cares of a troublesome world and ever at rest. Yet it's natural for man to want to live & I wish so to do in this case, if it is the will of the good Lord to spare me. I want to see the end of this war, let the end be what it may. I want to see it and see it soon. If they continue furloughing men, I am going to try to get off the last of this month if I can—if Col. Lowe & Maj. Stowe come back able for duty—which I hope they will do. They are due here the 17th. I have a great desire to come home & see you all and to stay, if it was allowed.

[No date, no location]

If the enemy does not advance on us here, I think the furloughing will be kept up. If there had been any other field officer with the Regt., I could have come home before this time, but I am, under the circumstances, compelled to stay. I have the largest Regt. in this army that has been in the service as long as it has and had as few conscripts in it as it has had. Also, it stands high now for its discipline & good behavior, which I take as quite a compliment, as it has been under my command alone for over two months, and my personal command for over ⅔ of the time since I came back. If I have got an enemy in it, I do not know who he is. I have now 453 privates & 27 officers present & came from Penn. with only 118 men. O, if they could live to get home.

You sent me a receipt from old man Hutchins for $40 which you have paid. You have paid him that much over the $100 which he was to have. Is that correct that you have paid the $40 & $20 making $60 over the $100 or is the $60 all that you have paid? You recollect I paid him $50 myself at Rapidan last May 1862. If you have only paid in all $60, then he has had $10 over his pay. If you have paid $160, then with the $50 I paid him, he has had $110 over his pay. When you write, let me know how much you paid his father in all. I wrote James a mild kind letter. I would be glad if he would let you and Mother see it. My love to my dear Mother and you and love to James & may he do better for time to come.

Asbury

Near Or. [Orange C.H.] 28th NC Regt.
January 26, 1864

My Ever Dear Brother James

I was very agreeably surprised last evening to get a very kind letter from you by Dr. Dozier. I was very happy to receive it, for it was a long time ago, it seems like, since I got a letter from you.

I have but little news to write to you. I am in most excellent health, except [for] a very severe cough that I have had all the fall & winter. I am more fleshy than I have been since I was sick at Wilmington. I am sometimes uneasy about my cough, but I suppose it is nothing serious. The reason for my being so fleshy, I think, is that I have been living very well for the last month & half.

There has been a large amount of good things coming from home to the men and you know that I am certain to buy some when money will bring it, although it is so high. The men are very kind to me. They frequently send me a part [of] what they get from home. By the way, I have been living very well & am so much like a horse that I always show my keeping. I have rheumatism very much sometimes. My Regt. is living very high now. I never have known so much provisions coming to the army in my life—hundreds of boxes & loads of them every day coming to the Regt.

Well, Jim, I can't tell you how little I think of our Congress. I do think of all the weak bodies of men that I ever read after that this is the weakest for a legislative one. As you say, it seems that they will never be satisfied till every body is in the army. I would like to know how they do expect for us to live with all the men in the army. If Congress would devise means to keep all the men that are on the muster rolls in the army & make them do their duty, and put all the provisional guards in the army that they have in the cities & towns, that are doing no good, only Devil, [then] honest citizens [would not be] coming to see their friends & to protect thieves. And also put all the able-bodied men in the army that they have in the peace departments with the enrolling offices & let their duties be performed by disabled officers & men (of which there is plenty), and also equip & furnish the men in the field better, we would have an army sufficient to keep back the Yankees.

For we now have more men in the field than we can take care of well. If they would do what they ought to do for the currency, we might think then of success, but no, they must whip us by the currency & starvation. The Yankees can never whip us if everybody would do what is right, but I do fear that will never be done. I fear the poor people will suffer at home & I must confess, I see but little prospect of peace soon, unless something does turn up soon.

I suppose you have a negro boy to help you work. If you have not, I think Father ought to get one, as there is plenty of them to hire & you have plenty of land to tend & it ought to be tended. I would advise you to get one. I hope you will not have to come to the army & will be able to keep out, for I never want any more of my people in it. I do want to see you all very much. I want to see Mother, Father, & Aunt so much that I can't hardly stand it, as well as you & Vet. I am certain I will get home by March Court, as I will certainly have a field officer for daily duty before that time. I am going to send up a furlough to be used when I have a field officer for duty.

Tell Mother to send me a cake of soap by Evan Reece. Tell her I am thankful for the nice sausage she sent me by Smith [Dozier]. I will eat it & think of you all. I have got half of that fine cheese she sent me yet. Give my love to Mother, Father & Aunt & accept the same yourself. May the good Lord bless us all & take care of us & let us all meet after this war in peace—your affectionate Brother—write soon.

W. H. A. Speer

[In a February 5, 1864, letter to Captain E. J. Hale, Jr., Asbury expressed his devotion to the Southern cause. However, in a February 18 letter to his father, Asbury said there is "some national sin hanging over us." Once again, Asbury is torn by conflicting loyalties. Asbury's letters, as well as the resolutions

of Company C, Twenty-Eighth Regiment, N.C.T., are included here.]

RESOLUTIONS OF THE TWENTY-EIGHTH
NORTH CAROLINA REGIMENT.
HEADQUARTERS, TWENTY-EIGHTH N.C.T.,
February 5th, 1864

Captain,—Complying with the request of the officers and men of the Twenty-eighth regiment, it gives me pleasure to report to General Lane that his gallant old regiment—knowing that the term of service for which it re-organized under his command will expire in September next, and believing that the cause in which it then enlisted so cheerfully, is just and righteous, and that it still demands the undivided efforts of all—has resolved to re-enlist for the war, adopting the resolutions of Company C, which are enclosed herewith.

I only embody the universal sentiment of the Twenty-eighth North Carolina regiment, when I express the hope that the kindly relations, which have heretofore existed between it and its original Colonel, may be perpetuated, and that he may be spared to command us to the close of the war.

I am, Captain, very respectfully,
Your obedient servant,
W. H. A. Speer,
Lieutenant-Colonel Commanding,
Captain E. J. Hale, Jr.,[16]
Assistant Adjutant-General.

RESOLUTIONS OF COMPANY C,
TWENTY-EIGHTH N.C.T.

At a meeting held in Company C, Twenty-eighth North Carolina troops, January 30, 1864, Captain

---

[16]As Assistant Adjutant General for the Lane Brigade, Captain E. J. Hale, Jr., was in charge of correspondence, keeping records, and dispensing orders.

James Monroe Grice
Served in Company C (Catawba) of 28th Regiment N.C.T.
Promoted to Sergeant in May of 1863. Wounded at Freder-
icksburg, Chancellorsville, and Gettysburg. His great
granddaughter, Margaret Eggers of Boone, N. C., has the
Civil War diary of Sergeant Grice. (Photo from Clark, N. C.
Regiments, 1901.)

T. J. Linebarger was called to the chair, and Corporal G. A. Abernethy appointed secretary.

The object of the meeting having been explained by the President, Lieutenant M. A. Throneburg, and privates J. M. Grice[17] and J. P. Little were appointed a committee to draft resolutions expressive of the sentiments of the meeting.

Lieutenant Throneburg from the Committee on Resolutions reported and read the following preamble and resolutions which were unamously [sic] adopted:

WHEREAS, The term of service for which we enlisted will expire in August next, and whereas, the exigencies of the services demand of every soldier to remain at his post and to do battle for his country's rights; therefore, be it

Resolved, By the officers and men of Company C, Twenty-eighth North Carolina troops, that we, believing our cause to be a holy and just one, do hereby pledge ourselves to re-enlist for the war; and do further declare our intention never to lay down our arms or abandon the struggle till our Government shall be recognized, our soil freed from the invader, our liberties secured, and peace restored to our bleeding country.

Resolved, That we earnestly request a general convention of the regiment to meet on Monday, February 1st, 1864.

Resolved, That the secretary communicate a copy of these resolutions to Brigadier-General Lane; also a copy to Colonel Speer, with the request that they be published on parade this afternoon.

On motion the meeting adjourned.

T. J. Linebarger, President
G. A. Abernethy, Secretary[18]

---

[17]James Monroe Grice served in Company C (Catawba County) of the 28th Regiment, N.C.T. He was wounded at Fredericksburg, Chancellorsville, and Gettysburg. He was pronoted to Sergeant in May of 1863. His great granddaughter, Margaret Eggers, of Boone, North Carolina, has the Civil War diary of Sergeant Grice. N. C. Troops, Vol. VIII, pp. 110-111.
[18]SHSP, Vol. 9, pp. 357-359.

N. a Or. 28. N.C.T.
Feb. 18, 1864

Ever Dear Father

I received your kind & interesting letter by Evan & was truly glad to hear from you, also to see that you had changed your notion about writing. As you say, your letters are some-times gloomy, yet I am always proud to get your letters, for I know when I read them that I am reading honest sentiments, that you only express what you believe, [and] if mistaken, it is honestly so. But, Father, I have long been of the opinion that things are likely to turn out as you think, unless there is a speedy change for the better.

We certainly have had as weak a Congress as ever was assembled, and I am truly glad that its time is out today. For we cannot be worsted by the new. I have always been opposed to any further conscription of men to go to the army. There is no doubt but what we have men enough to keep back the enemy, if the men who belong to the army were made to stay with the army & do their duty. And they at home, the men who are at home, made to cultivate the soil & make bread & meat for the army & wives & children of the soldiers. Also, if Congress would provide & equip the men that they have in the field, as they ought to do, our army then would be as efficient as an army could be made. The men would be better clad, better fed and, in every respect, better qualified to do their duty &, at the same time, knowing that their families at home were not suffering for the necessaries of life.

I can't picture to you the suffering that many of our men have gone through with, for the want of clothes, shoes and other comforts that might be furnished them. Also, Congress ought to try to do something for our currency. I think that their legislation on that is very lame but the most alarming thing is about something to eat. I awfully fear that the women and children of the poor class of men will come to suffer.

There is something wrong somewhere. We have as brave & great an army as ever went on a battle field, but there is some national sin hanging over us & I fear it is the nigger. So far as I am concerned, I would be glad if every drop of nigger blood was out of the Confederacy. If it was not for the nigger, this war, I think, would close in less than 60 days from today. For it has come down to the nigger as the great difficulty that is in the way. And I believe if the South was to agree to emancipate all the slaves in 30 years that the war would close at once &, for my part, I am in favor of it, but this, you know, would [not] do for me to say to anyone else yet.

I don't think the war can last much longer, let things go as they will. I believe I will be spared to outlive the whole of it, and I am determined if I live, to tell the people what I think of secession & those who advocate it. I am against the doctrine & against those who are for it—against monarchy or a despotism, either military or political. The people ought to rule & the old men's council ought to be taken in place of that of younger heads heated up with mean whiskey.

I will stop here & talk the matter over when I come home. I can't say at what time I will be at home, but sometime in March I have a furlough for 30 days to be used as soon as a field officer returns to the Regt. I am looking for one soon. I will come as soon as I can. I am sorry things at home are as they are. I hope that they will certainly do better. I am very thankful for the leather & soap by Evan. Capt. Bohannon, Snow & many of the men send you their respects. Express my love to you & Mother, also to James & Aunt. Tell Aunt I will write to her soon. May the good Lord take care of us all is the prayer of your son.

W. H. A. Speer

N. a Or. 28. N.C.T.
April 4 1864

Dear Father & Mother

I got to camp safe after a long tedious journey and found the men very well & all glad to see me. I have no news of any importance. It is expected that there will be fighting here as soon as the roads get dry. It has been snowing again & is raining also, & is likely for rain again. Gov. Vance has been

In a February 18, 1864, letter to his father, Asbury said, "There is some national sin hanging over us." He also said, "I am determined, if I live, to tell the people what I think of secession and those who advocate it."

here & made us a fine speech. [It] pleased the men very much. I think he takes the proper view of the subject. He is for negotiations for peace & stopping the war as soon as it can be done. He has no idea of fighting till we retake Ky. Me.O, [Missouri?] leave that for negotiations here after. I went with him to Gordonsville.

Well, Father & Mother, I enjoyed my visit at home very much. It was very pleasant for me to be with you all. It is the next place to heaven to be with my Dear Father, Mother, Aunt & Brothers at home. Even in times of war, [it] is delightful & Oh! what would it be if peace was declared. I shall look back to my visit at home with great pleasure & delight.

But it was the greatest trial for me to part with you all that I have ever had to undergo in my life, although I maned [manned] up under it the best I could. I trust if the good Lord will spare my life to get home again, that I will never have to leave again to go [to] the war. I humbly trust the good Lord will spare my life to get home again & I believe he will. I spoke to Gov. Vance about the constables, magistrates & militia officers being conscripted. He told me he should not give them up but was going to keep them at home, which will save James, & I am glad of it. I hope you will have a good time for planting, etc. Write—my love to you both & to James & Aunt. May the good Lord preserve us to meet at home again.

Your son, W. H. A. Speer

P.S.

Tell Old Rachill that the letters she told me about was here when I come, just as she said. I almost think she has hit it, at least she has so far. I hope that part of it about my getting home again safe is so.

The Dying Soldier

I am dying, comrade, dying,
Ebbs the feeble life-tide fast,
And the dark mysterious shadows,
Gather on the evening blast,

Raise heads, dear friends and listen,
To the few, faint words I speak,
Hear the last wish of a soldier,
Eno [even though] life's pulses grow too weak,

Though I came with Southern freemen,
With brave hearts and arms of might,
Gainst the foe's invading legion,
To defend our homes and right,

Though I cannot, mid the battle,
Feel my heart's exulting thrill,
Yet, I perish like a soldier,
Die a Southern patriot still,   I

Tell my noble gray-haired Father,
Here beside Potomac's wave,
That his son, his pride, his darling,
Fills a soldier's honored grave,

Tell him that the Christian's armor,
Sword of faith and shield of love,
Won my way of life eternal,
To a peaceful home above,

Tell my mother that my spirit,
Dreads not God's all-righteous frown,
That I passed to heaven triumphant,
Bore the cross and won the crown,

I am dying, comrade, dying,
Tell my heart's last fitfull swell,
Tell the cold dew gathering o'er me,
Father, Mother, friends — Farewell.

    Written by me near Liberty
    Mills at camp for my Dear Father,

Mother, Brothers and Aunt in event
I fall in the Army May the 1st 1864.[19]

*[Four days after Asbury wrote "The Dying Soldier," the Army of
the Potomac launched its spring offensive. Beginning with the
Battle of the Wilderness, General Grant attempted a series of
flanking moves toward Richmond, hoping to bring Lee into*

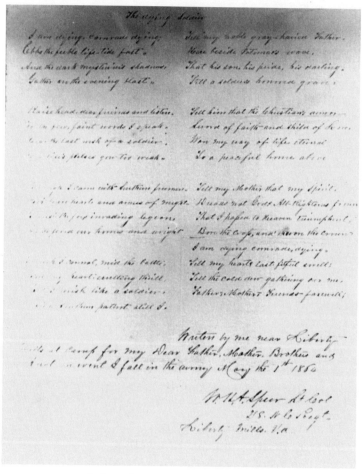

Asbury's poem — "The Dying Soldier"

---

[19]The Battle of the Wilderness started on May 5, 1864.

open country where he could be attacked. *This series of moves around Lee's right flank continued until Grant reached the Weldon Railroad south of Petersburg, where he hoped to cut off Lee's communication with the South. Asbury's regiment was defending the Weldon Railroad when he was mortally wounded on August 25, 1864. From the Wilderness to Reams' Station, a span of nearly four months, Asbury faced a seemingly endless series of fights and marches, pausing only to assemble fortifications and breastworks. For Asbury, the final months of his life were the ultimate test of human endurance and faith. His experiences are well documented in three battle reports written during this time.[20] These battle reports are interspersed with Asbury's letters in order to provide an accurate chronology.]*

Headquarters 28th N.C.T.
July 19th 1864

Capt. E. J. Hale, Jr.
A.A.Gen'l

I beg leave to make the following report of the part taken by my Reg't in the different engagements commencing May 5th up to July 2nd 1864. The Reg't has been in so many different battles, skirmishes, etc. in this campaign that you will excuse me for condensing my report, also for including them in one.

My Reg't left camp at Liberty Mills, where we had spent the winter, on the 4th of May/64. With the Brigade we marched down the Plank Road leading to Fredericksburg and camped for the night near the battlefield of Mine Run. We left camp early next morning 5th May and continued our march down the Plank Road. About 10 a.m. skirmishing commenced in our front and to the right of the road. We marched on and [were] soon skirmishing on the left of the road. I received orders from Gen'l Lane to deploy skirmishers on the left of

[20]Reports of William Henry Asbury Speer for the Twenty-Eighth Regiment N.C.T., 19 July 1864, and 31 July 1864 in folders 73 and 74, James Henry Lane Papers, Auburn University, and Report of S. N. Stowe, 28 August 1864, Folder 77, Lane Papers, Auburn University.

the road to protect my Reg't.

As we moved on in this manner, I moved forward till I came into a field nearby, where the Battle of the Wilderness was fought. Here my Regiment filed off to the left along a country road, through some fields, across a little stream into a piece of woods. [We] halted [and] formed line of battle, my Reg't being on the right of the Brigade. My left, resting on the right of the 18th N.C.T., we moved forward through a piece of woods and assisted in capturing some 150 or 200 prisoners. I then moved by the left flank after the Brigade back to the road until I came near to the Plank Road, where I inclined to the left and struck the Plank Road near the battlefield.

By order of Gen'l Lane I countermarched my Reg't. [I] filed to the right of the Plank Road through the woods after the 18th N.C.T. Having gone some distance in this easterly direction, I halted and formed line of battle with my right on the left of the 18th N.C.T and my left on the right of the 33rd N.C.T. I here got orders from Gen'l Lane that when my Reg't came to Gen'l McGowan's[21] Brigade in line, that I would halt.

The fighting in front was now very heavy. I moved forward with the Brigade [and] came to Gen'l. Scales[22] line of battle, which was now engaged with the enemy. My Regiment gallantly moved forward down the line in front and immediately opened upon the enemy a most destructive fire, driving everything in front of the Regiment. I continued to press my men forward through an almost impenetrable swamp of mud, briars and bushes. My men charged forward driving the enemy from his third line of defense, having by this time passed beyond the swamp in face of a terrific fire from the

---

[21]General John McGowan, a South Carolina lawyer and politician before the war, was wounded at the Battle of Spotsylvania Court House. He was also wounded in the Peninsular Campaign, at Second Bull Run and at Chancellorsville. "He continued in the Army of Northern Virginia until Appomattox. After the war he was a legislator and associate justice of the S. C. Supreme Court." Boatner's Dictionary, p. 533.

[22]General Alfred M. Scales was a graduate of the University of North Carolina at Chapel Hill. He was a Colonel of the 13th Regiment N.C.T. before being appointed Brigadier General on June 13, 1863. "He commanded his own brigade under General Wilcox at the Wilderness and during the Petersburg siege. After the war he was a lawyer, congressman, banker, and Governor of North Carolina." Boatner's Dictionary, p. 724.

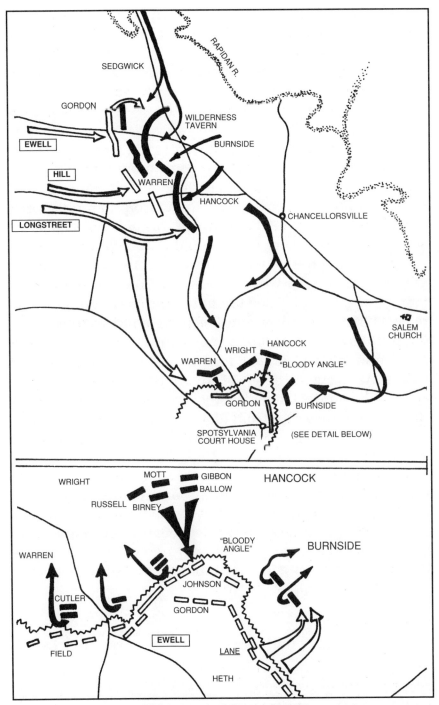

Wilderness and Spotsylvania

enemy, [but still] driving him at all points. I was here informed by Capt. Lovell and Adj't Folger[23] that I had no support on my right flank and that the enemy was firing into my flank. And seeing I was 200 yards in front of my support on my left flank, I halted my Reg't at the works above mentioned. My men still continued to give the enemy their destructive fire.

By this time it was quite dark and my men were out of ammunition. I ordered them to procure ammunition from the dead and wounded, which was done. I then, finding I had no support and the enemy just in my front in strong force, ordered my Reg't to fall back, which was done in good order, some 150 yards where I halted and reformed. I put out my scouts, at which time the Adj't of the 33rd N.C.T. came to see who I was, after which Col. Avery brought up his Reg't (33rd N.C.T.) and formed on mine. In this condition, I sent to Gen'l Lane for orders, but before I got orders from him, I found the enemy cautiously moving up in heavy force. Col Avery and myself fell back further and halted and awaited orders. At this point, about 11 o'clock p.m., we got ordered to come and join the balance of the Brigade then on the Plank Road, where we arrived and took our position in line among the rest of the Reg'ts of the Brigade, where the men spent the night.

In this battle I cannot say too much for my men and officers, each seemed to vie with his companions in arms and deeds of valor. My Regiment went further than any other had gone or did go. It never did better. Capt. Lovell of Co. "A" acted as my major and did his part nobly. My Adjutant, R. S. Folger, acted very gallantly throughout all the action. Likewise [for] my company officers.

May the sixth (6th)

This morning found us all "closed in mass," the 18th &

---

[23]Romulus S. Folger served as Lieutenant in Company I (Yadkin County) of the 28th Regiment N.C.T. before being appointed Adjutant on January 7, 1863. He was present when Lee surrendered at Appomattox Court House on April 9, 1865. N. C. Troops, Vol. VIII, pp. 110-111.

37th N. C. were in front, with the 7th N. C. between my Reg't and the front line above mentioned. Gen. Scales Brigade, being in line of battle in the front, was suddenly attacked by an overwhelming force and gave way. This caused a stampede among the troops in [the] rear, causing the whole [brigade] to fall back in rather a disorderly manner. However, with the assistance of my officers I succeeded in reforming my Regiment some distance back on the Plank Road. When the Brigade was formed, I then moved back on the Plank Road with the Brigade, took the left, and went into the field where we went before the battle of the 5th. Here we spent the remainder of the day in fortifying a new line. On this line my Reg't slept for the night.

May 7th. This day was spent in strengthening our line and shifting positions.

May 8th. This morning, it being ascertained that the enemy was moving to our right, we commenced moving about 2 p.m. and marched till late in the night when we camped and cooked rations before day.

May 9th. We took up line of march early this morning and arrived at 4 at Spotsylvania. At 12 we formed line of battle, my right resting on the 18th N. C. and my left on Gen'l Walker's Brigade.

May 10th. This morning our Brigade moved along the line, my left resting in an angle of the works, and on the right of Gen'l R. D. Johnston's Brigade.[24] My right [was] still upon the 18th N. C. This Brigade moved to the left during the day, at which time I also moved to the left, with my left resting at an elbow of the works at the top of a hill. Here the Reg't spent the day, until late in the evening when it was moved into the Brigade by the right flank up the road to near where the lines were broken by an assault of the enemy. But not being

---

[24]Robert Johnston was appointed Brigadier General on September 1, 1863, and commanded a brigade under General Rodes at the Battle of the Wilderness in May of 1864. He was severely wounded at Spotsylvania Court House but later fought at Petersburg and Appomattox. After the war he practiced law. Boatner's Dictionary, pp. 441-442.

needed, we moved back to our old position and rested for the night.

May 11th. Today my Reg't moved to the left through lines and skirmished until late into the day. Late in the day it rested in a line of old works across a ravine, then we slept for the night.

May 12th. This morning found my Reg't in the works at an early hour, with my left resting on Gen. Steuart's[25] right. Gen. Lane rode up the line at daylight and as Johnston's Division was attacked, he told me that I must hold my position and then rode to the right of my Reg't. This was just at the dawn of day when Gen'l Johnston was attacked. His lines were instantly broken, which let the enemy to my rear, as well as to my front. I found the troops on my left flying in utter confusion in every direction. [I] found the enemy coming down the works on both sides. I hastened to the right of my Reg't and informed Gen'l Lane of the facts. He ordered me to move out my Reg't. by the right flank. I hastened to the left [to] give the order [to] my men still in the works. By this time, the enemy, being on both sides, my Reg't left as best they could. Here I lost 113 men as prisoners. I succeeded in rallying a portion of my men with Col. Cowan's[26] in an arm of the works to the right, on top of the hill. Here took place one of the most desperate fights of the war. The stubborn fight made here by Lane's Brigade certainly saved the day. And I am happy to say that my Reg't did her part well.

After the fighting at this place was over, I moved to the right with the Brigade on a line running North from the Brick Kiln. Here I was not able to get on the line for want of room. My Reg't was in reserve until late in the evening, when the

[25]An Indian fighter, George H. "Maryland" Steuart "commanded an infantry brigade at Gettysburg, the Wilderness, and Spotsylvania, where he was captured in the Bloody Angle. After the war he farmed in Maryland." Boatner's Dictionary, p. 796.
[26]Robert V. Cowan first served as Captain of Company A, 33rd Regiment N.C.T. He was later promoted to Colonel on June 18, 1864, following the death of Colonel Clark M. Avery, who was mortally wounded at Wilderness. When the order came to surrender his regiment on April 10, 1865, he adamantly refused, and promptly mounted his horse and rode away. N. C. Troops,Vol. IX, p. 118.

Brigade moved in front of the works with Gen'l Mahone's[27] to take a battery. A line of battle was formed with Lane's Brigade in front in a piece of woods. My Reg't was on the left of the Brigade, my right resting on the 18th N. C. We moved by the right flank to the proper positions, when we were halted, fronted and moved forward. In this charge my Reg't behaved most gallantly. Some of the guns would not fire having been rained upon in the morning, but the men charged ahead with the bayonet. Many of my men were very close to the battery when Gen'l Lane gave the order to fall back. My Regiment took more prisoners than I had men engaged. Lieutenants L. A. Todd[28] and J. M. Starling,[29] the former of Co. "I," the latter of Co. "F" were captured with several recruits, and then retaken by our own men, capturing their captors. Some of my men fought with anything they could get hold of.

The Regiment then came out to the works in front of the Court House. Here we reformed again and moved to the works then vacated for us, with my right on the left of the 33rd N. C. and my left on the 37th N. C. Here we drew rations and rested for the night, which was very desirable after as hard a days work as we had done.

May 13th. This morning we moved to the left along the line some distance, where we halted and spent the day strengthening our works. The 14th, 15th and 16th were in like manner. On the night of the 16th my Regiment was relieved by one of Gen'l McGowan's Regiments, after which I moved my Regiment to the rear of the second line near the Brick Kiln and rested for the night. The 18th was spent in this position. On the 19th I moved to the left with the Brigade and formed on a second line as support for Gen'l

---

[27]The son of a tavernkeeper, William Mahone would later become an engineer and superintendent of a railroad. "He fought at Fredericksburg, Chancellorsville, Gettysburg, the Wilderness, and Spotsylvania before being named Major General 30 July 1864 in an on-the-spot promotion by Lee for his performance at the Petersburg crater." After the war he was, once again, president of a railroad. He was elected to the U. S. Senate in 1880. Boatner's Dictionary, p. 502.

[28]L. A. Todd served in Company I (Yadkin County) of the 28th Regiment N.C.T. He was elected 3rd Lieutenant on October 20, 1863. He was at Appomattox Court House when Lee surrendered to Grant on April 9, 1865. N. C. Troops, Vol. VIII, p. 207.

[29]James M. Starling mustered in as private and was promoted to Sergeant January-June 1862. He was appointed 3rd Lieutenant on May 11, 1863. N. C. Troops, Vol. VIII, p. 174.

Gorden.[30] My left [was] resting on the right of the 18th, while my right [was] on the 33rd N.C.T. Here I fortified under heavy shelling. On the 19th we moved back to the right into the field to await orders, when Gen'l Ewell[31] was on his flank move. At dark my Reg't, being on the left of the Brigade, moved by the left flank along the works to the extreme left of the line, to a portion of the works then vacated by Gen'l Ewell's Corps, where I spent the night. Before day, on the morning of the 20th, we moved back to the right and spent the day. On the 21st we moved back to the right to the position on the line occupied formerly by Gen'l Gordon's Brigade. From this position we moved by the right flank along the works to a church south of the Court House, where we filed to the left, passed beyond the works, formed line of battle, with my right on the road, my left resting on 33rd N.C.T. and charged through the woods capturing the Yankee breastworks. In this charge my men acted well. I lost Lieutenant Ed. S. Edwards[32] Co. "G," one of my best officers. My Reg't then came out to the road at the church and moved down the road toward the Central R. R. above Hanover Junction. We marched till 2 o'clock a.m.

On the morning of the 22nd the line of march was assumed at 4½ o'clock a.m. and was kept up at a very rapid gait, until the Central R. R. was reached. Here we took up camp near Bramlett's Station, eight miles above the junction.

On the morning of the 23rd the march resumed moving along the R. R. to near Anderson's Crossing, when we filed to the left with the Brigade and went in close to the River, where the Reg't rested. In the evening, when it moved up the

[30]General John Brown Gorden, after graduating from the University of Georgia, became super-intendent of a coal mine in Alabama. During the war, "he commanded a Georgia brigade at Chancellorsville, Gettysburg, the Wilderness, and Spotsylvania before being named Major General 14 May 1864." After the war he was the Governor of Georgia and a U. S. Senator. Boatner's Dictionary, pp. 348-349.

[31]A veteran of the Mexican War and an Indian fighter, Richard Stoddert Ewell would later command a division under Stonewall Jackson. After Jackson's death, Ewell became commander of the II Corps. Having lost a leg at Groveton, "he was lifted on his horse and strapped in his saddle to lead the advance into Pennsylvania.... He led his corps at the Wilderness and Spotsylvania until a fall from his horse at the "bloody angle" left him unfit for further service." Boatner's Dictionary, pp. 268-269.

[32]A native of Orange County, Edward S. Edwards served in Company G of the 28th Regiment N.C.T. He was promoted to 1st Lieutenant on July 19, 1863, and was killed at Spotsylvania Court House on May 21, 1864. N. C. Troops, Vol. VIII, p. 185.

R. R. with the Brigade, it formed line of battle, with my left resting upon Gen'l McGowen's right, the line at right angles with the R. R. The enemy not advancing here, the Reg't then moved by the left flank up the R. R. and formed in battle order parallel to the R. R., my left on Gen'l McGowan's. The Reg't then moved forward, drove in the enemies pickets and attacked the enemies main line in the woods, where the Reg't fought till dark closed the scene. The Reg't displayed its usual good conduct. We then fell back to the farm at the edge of the woods with the rest of the Brigade, where we rested until relieved by one of Gen. Davis'[33] Reg'ts (of Heth's Div). My Reg't moved back to the R. R. with the Brigade, halted for a while, then moved down the R. R. with the Brigade to the Anderson house and halted for the remainder of the night.

On the 24th May the Reg't built heavy breastworks. On the 25th the Reg't moved back, fortified, and was under a very heavy fire from shelling. On the 26th it remained in the same position. On the 27th of May, at 2 p.m., the Reg't moved off by the Ashland road, marched till 10 p.m. and camped for the night, within one mile of Ashland. On the 28th we marched very rapidly all day, took up camp east of Atlee's Station on the Va. Central Railroad, within two miles of Mechanicsville. On 29th, late in the day, the Reg't moved back with the Brigade and camped near Gen'l Heth's Division. On the 30th the Reg't formed the line of battle, my left resting on the 18th N. C., my right on the 33rd N. C. Here the Reg't threw up strong lines of works. On the 31st the Reg't moved to the right [and] took position in a line of works, my right on General Thomas'[34] Brigade, my left on the 37th N. C. Here the Regiment was exposed to a most terrific shelling and did heavy skirmishing all day. I lost five men. At night the Reg't moved back with the Brigade to a second line and fortified. June 1st was spent behind the works. The men were

---

[33]General Robert Joseph Davis was the nephew of Confederate President Jefferson Davis. "He led a brigade of Mississippi Troops in the Army of Northern Virginia, fighting at Gettysburg, the Wilderness, Cold Harbor, and the battles around Petersburg." After the surrender at Appomattox he assumed the practice of law. Boatner's Dictionary, pp. 226-227.
[34]A native of Georgia, General Edward L. Thomas fought at Fredericksburg, Chancellorsville, Gettysburg, the Wilderness, Spotsylvania, Petersburg, and Appomattox. He was a graduate of Emory College and a wealthy plantation owner. Boatner's Dictionary, pp. 835-836.

glad to get rest, as they had worked all night.

June 2nd we took up line of march by the right flank and marched to Gaine's Mill. Here we fortified, then moved by the right flank to the right of General Breckinridge's[35] Division, when the Reg't formed line of battle, charged and took ____ Ridge. We formed [a new] line of battle with my right on Gen'l Thomas' Brigade, my left on the 37th N. C. Here the Reg't threw up strong works. From this time up to June the 13th at eight o'clock a.m. was spent in these works, making them stronger and making [ourselves] as comfortable as the nature of the case would permit. From sharp shooters at this place I lost two men killed and five men wounded by enfilade shots.

[At Cold Harbor, on June 3, 1864, Grant's frontal assault against Lee was a total disaster. The attack, which lasted eight minutes, was turned back with a loss of 7,000 Union soldiers. "More men fell in this short period of time than in any other like period of time during the entire war."[36]]

8 A.M. Cold Harbor June 5/64

My Ever Dear Father & Mother, Aunt & Bros.

I write you today a short line. Thank the good Lord I am well & alive. We have been fighting the enemy here on the old battle ground of June 28 & 29/62. On the 3rd they assaulted our lines all along, but were repulsed with great slaughter. It is said their loss was, that day, over 10,000. They have got to fighting of a night. Last night they were firing more or less all night. We can't sleep any. Our loss here is very slight so far. We have fought behind breastworks.[37] It is raining on us & quite disagreeable. The men are getting sick very fast & I don't wonder at it, for they have gone through with so much. I am almost give out. I wonder at my holding up as well as I do.

---

[35]Before the war, General John Breckinridge was a politician, serving as Buchanan's vice president and later running for president against Abraham Lincoln. "He later commanded a division at Cold Harbor." Boatner's Dictionary, pp. 82-83.

[36]Boatner's Dictionary, pp. 162-165.

[37]Breastworks are fortified trenches. World War I would be fought in this manner.

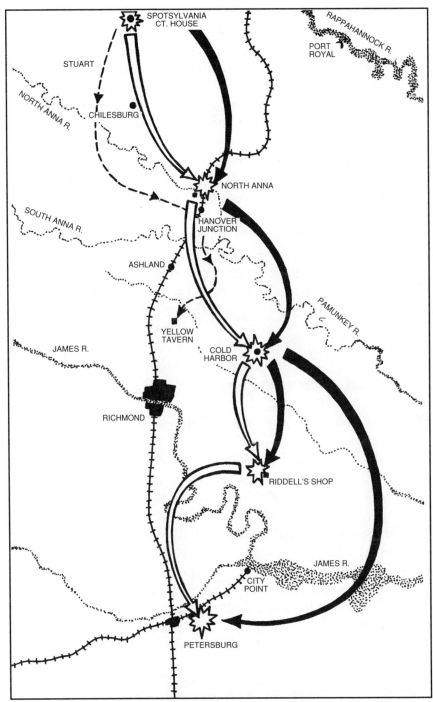

From Spotsylvania to Petersburg

— 137 —

This is 32 days we have been fighting & I have been under fire every day in the time, except about 4 days. I have never seen anything like this in my life, but I will not grumble, if my life will only be spared. I am so thankful that the good Lord has thus far not left me. It must be in answer to the prayers of my Dear parents, Aunt, & friends. I pray [for] the good Lord to protect me & I have committed my soul to His care. I know He will preserve & protect me & do with me according to His good pleasure. If we will only have faith, all will be right.

Genl. Lane[38] was seriously wounded on the 3rd. Tell the neighbors their boys are all well. Oh, Father & Mother, I want to live to see you all again. Certainly this war will soon close. Such slaughter can't be stood long. Pray for me. All accept my love — may the good Lord take care of us all — write.

Your son, Asbury

[Colonel Speer's battle report continues]

On the 13th at 8 a.m., my Reg't took up the line of march crossing the Chichahomany at McCellan's Bridge, continued the march across the York River R. R. to the Charles City road, where the Reg't filed down the road to the left. [We then] marched some distance [and] formed line of battle at right angles to the road, in support of Gen'l Scales' Brigade. [We] moved forward some distance, then moved by the right flank and filed to the left down the road, [then] filed to the right, formed line again and moved forward as support to Gen'l McGowan's Brigade. My Regiment, on the extreme right of our Brigade, moved forward till I came up [even] with McGowan's Brigade. [We then] filed to the right and formed line of battle with the Brigade and commenced fortifying.

From this position the Regiment moved forward in a charge some mile and a half. After dark my right came in close proximity to the enemy's line. Here I was ordered by the Brigade commander to halt and deflect back my Regiment

[38]While General James Henry Lane was recovering from wounds received in battle, June 3, his brigade was commanded at different times by Colonel John Barry, Colonel Asbury Speer, and General Conner.

to protect the flank of the Brigade, which was done. Some time in the night the Reg't moved back to the left flank and took position formerly occupied by it near Mr. Nelson's house. In this position we spent the 14th.

On the 15th of June I moved with my Reg't with the Brigade to the front, on a new line to the left of Gen'l Thomas, with my right resting on his left. [We then] fortified a main line. On the 16th I moved back to my old position at Nelson's house. On the 17th at 4 p.m. the Reg't took up the line of march for Darbytown, where we camped for the night. Early on the 18th the Reg't commenced the march for Petersburg, and arriving at Petersburg at 6 o'clock p.m. The Regiment performed one of the hardest and most disagreeable marches it ever has. We passed through the city to the works South of the city nearby, and on the east side of the Railroad, and rested for the night.

On the 19th I took position in the works, then moved to the left until my left rested on Gen'l Mahone's right, my right on the 18th N.C.T. Here we remained till the 21st, when the Reg't moved by the right flank out the Railroad and marched down the road. At dark the Reg't moved back to its former position.

On the 22nd the Reg't moved again to the right and front to help execute a flank move upon the enemy. After marching some distance, it halted, formed line of battle, moved forward through as many natural difficulties as I ever saw. [We] soon came on the enemy skirmishers, fought them, drove them, and took some 40 prisoners. [We] were under a heavy fire, in which I lost some good men. [We then] moved out of the woods by the left flank, formed in a field, was under heavy shelling, then moved forward to support General Wright's[39] Brigade, then engaged from this place. After dark the Reg't moved back to its position.

On the morning of the 23rd my Reg't moved by the left flank along the works to relieve a portion of General Finni-

---

[39]A Georgia lawyer before the war, General Ambrose Wright would later command a brigade at Fredericksburg, Chancellorsville, Gettysburg, and the Wilderness. After the war he became a newspaper editor. "He died soon after being elected to Congress." Boatner's Dictionary, p. 949.

gan's[40] Brigade. In going to my position I suffered much. My Reg't deserves much praise for the manner in which it took its place in this very disagreeable and dangerous position. My Regiment held till the 26th, when I was relieved by one of General McGowan's Regiments. My men suffered here from almost everything, as well as shot and shell. I lost 7 men killed and 16 wounded — Captain James M. Crowell,[41] Co. "K," no braver man ever wielded a sword in defense of Southern rights, was killed in the still darkness of the night, about the hour of eleven. His life was sacrificed at the hands of a ruthless invader.

9 a.m. Petersburg June 25/64

My Dear Father & Mother

I write you a short line. I am, thank the good Lord, alive & tolerable & well. We were in a battle here on the 22nd. I lost in Co. I, killed, Wm. Stricklin, wounded, Abraham Stinson - in the heel & leg, severe. On the 23rd, Elias Stinson was killed [and] Henry Whitehead wounded. Capt. Crowell was killed last night instantly. I have had six men killed here & 9 wounded. There was tremendous artillery firing yesterday. Genl. Hoke made a charge yesterday & was repulsed. It is very strange to me that our Genls. will keep charging breastworks. If they get at it again, our army will soon be gone. We drove the enemy on the 22nd, took 1,600 prisoners, 8 stands of colors & 4 pieces of artillery. The works we are now in are so close to the enemy's lines we can't stick up our heads without getting shot at. We are in the open field. No shade's over us in the boiling sun & the hottest weather I ever did see & no rain. We have had no rain in over a month & it seems the heavens have dried up. I tell you, dear Father, it is horrible to be in this place. We are first shot down, day or night, any time. Our sharpshooters & the enemy are all the time

---

[40]A Florida lawyer beefore the war, General Joseph Finnigan was appointed Brigadier General on April 5, 1862. "He fought at Olustee and remained in the state until sent to Virginia with his brigade in May of 1864. There he led his forces at Cold Harbor and in the Petersburg siege, returning to Florida 20 March 1865. He was a lawyer again after the war." Boatner's Dictionary, p. 279.

[41]Captain James M. Crowell of Stanly County served in Company K of the 28th Regiment N.C.T. He was killed near Petersburg, Virginia, on June 24, 1864. N. C. Troops, Vol. VIII, p. 220.

James M. Crowell
Crowell served as Captain in Company K (Stanly County) of
the 28th Regiment N.C.T. In his Wilderness Battle Report,
Colonel Speer wrote, "No braver man ever wielded a sword
in defense of Southern rights." Speer went on to say he
"was killed in the still darkness of the night, about the
hour of eleven." James M. Crowell died near Petersburg,
Virginia, on June 24, 1864. (Photo from Clark, N. C. Regiments, 1901.)

looking for each other. As soon as a man shows his head he is plugged at & often killed or wounded. It is a perfect state of horror here. I am very thankful that I am yet alive. It looks like a wonder. The good Lord is so good to us. Oh! Father & Mother, let us praise His excellent name. My love to you both & to Aunt & James. I have wrote every few days & will so do if alive. Pray for me. May the good Lord bless us all & take care of us. God bless you all.

W. H. A. Speer

[The following paragraph concludes Colonel Speer's battle report that began on May 5, 1864.]

On the 24th I moved my Reg't out in the rear of the Brigade, then in General Connor's[42] position, where the Reg't rested till the 2nd of July, when it moved into the works. On the night of the 2nd of July my Reg't moved off and marched all night, crossing the James River at Chaffin's Bluff on the 3rd of July, and took position below the Bluff on a farm near Flour Mill Creek. Never has my Reg't displayed more conspicuous gallantry than in this campaign. Fighting and marching have been accomplished without mentioning fatigue, and privations have been admitted with patriotic endurance, as martyrs to the cause of freedom. I have to announce the names of Captain N. Clark[43] Co. "E," a Christian and patriot, Captain James M. Crowell Co. "K." a colossus of genuine bravery, Lieutenants E. S. Edwards Co. "G" and H. J. Castine Co. "B," both brave and gallant spirits, besides 32 enlisted men, with 121 wounded and 132 missing. Of the missing 113 were captured on the 12th May. Too much honor and praise cannot be bestowed upon my fine officers for their gallantry. I had no field officers to assist me in the campaign. Captains Lovell and Linebarger rendered valuable assistance to me and to my Adjutant, R. P. Folger, I

---

[42]A native of South Carolina, General James Connor was, before the war, a lawyer and a secessionist. During the war he "led the brigades of McGowan and Lane in succession, fighting at Riddle's Shop, Darby's Farm, Fussell's Mill, Petersburg, Jerusalem Plank Road, and Reams' Station." After the war, General Connor became Attorney General of South Carolina. Boatner's Dictionary, p. 171.

[43]Captain Niven Clark of Montgomery County served in Company E of the 28th Regiment N.C.T. He was killed at Spotsylvania Court House on May 12, 1864. N. C. Troops, Vol. VIII, p. 164.

Romulus S. Folger
Folger served as Lieutenant in Company I (Yadkin) of the
28th Regiment N.C.T. and was appointed Adjutant on January 7, 1863. He was present when Lee surrendered to
Grant at Appomattox Court House on April 9, 1865. (Photo
from Clark, N. C. Regiments, 1901.)

owe much and cannot do them the ample justice they so richly merit from me and their country. I am, Captain, very respectfully your obedient servant, W. H. A. Speer, Lt. Col. Commanding.

NCa Or. 28 N.C.T.

5 p.m. July 5/64

My Dear Father & Mother

I am happy to have the pleasure of writing you again. I trust you are all well. It has been so long since I heard from home. I am almost crazy. We are 3 miles below Chaffin's Bluff on the North side of the James. We came here on the night of the 2nd inst. from Petersburg. We were at Petersburg 3 weeks. The weather is awful hot & dry—no rain since the 12th of May—everything is nearly burnt up. If there had been only plenty of rain, the crops would have been fine. We would have had plenty of vegetables to eat. We did plenty of fighting at Petersburg. I lost 7 men killed, 15 wounded. Elias Stinson [and] Wm. Stricklin were killed. Abraham Stinson was wounded. I want you to tell Misses Stinson that I tried to get Abraham furloughed, so he could come home to harvest but I could not get it through. Well, Father, we are seeing sights marching, fighting & all sorts of hardships. Their gun boats are about 2½ miles from our lines. They throw shells over us here that weigh 180 lb., 2 ft. long, 15 in. through & look like churns. The enemy is on this side of the River in considerable force. It looks like the enemy is all around us in every direction. I am expecting more terrible fighting here. Our men are quite sickly here. I only have 220 men present for duty. [I] entered the campaign 4th [of] May with 525. I do hope you have good crops & plenty of vegetables to eat. I do wish I was with you to enjoy it. Tell my dear Mother to put up plenty of pickles. If I ever get home I will do them justice. I trust I have no opposition. If so, then I will be elected.[44] My respects to all, & love to all of you at home. I will look for a letter from some

---

[44]In the August 1864 election, William H. Asbury Speer was elected to the North Carolina Senate, defeating Colonel Horton of Boone.

of you soon. Tell Aunt Nancy - God bless you all.

Your son, Asbury

[This was the last known letter Colonel Speer wrote to his family.]

[Colonel W. H. A. Speer to Governor Vance, July 29, 1864, Vance Papers, North Carolina Division of Archives and History, Raleigh, North Carolina]

28th N. C.

July 29/64

Sir,

I have the honor & pleasure of writing that my Regt. voted as follows: Vance 179, Holden 31.[45] This vote is after a hard day's fight in which I have lost near 100 men. We had a river engagement with the cavalry. I am certain your election is certain, which I am very proud of. My election in 7 camps—all that are in the Regt.—is unanimous.

Respectfully, your friend

W. H. A. Speer, Col. 28th

If it had not been for the fight, your vote would have been much larger. I think I have done well, as several of my company are from Holden's counties.

[Battle Report]

Camp 28th NCT

July 31 1864

Capt. E. J. Hale Jr.

A.A.G.

I beg leave to make the following report of the part taken by my Reg't in the engagement of the 28th inst. My Reg't was formed in line of battle with my left on 37th N.C.T. [and my] right on the 33rd N.C.T. In this manuver my Reg't moved forward with the Brigade. In moving forward my Reg't came in contact with the enemy in a very thick swamp but drove them out into a cornfield. In getting through the swamp the

---

[45]William Holden, editor of the Raleigh <u>North Carolina Standard</u>, was badly defeated by Vance in the 1864 governor's race.

Reg't was broken up on formation to some extent, but reformed to some degree after getting into the cornfield. My men pressed the enemy through the cornfield under a fire, [with] the right of my Reg't passing along a fence moving to the southeast. My right flank was ____ before I crossed the swamp. After getting into the cornfield and passing through it into an open untended field, my Reg't was exposed very heavily to a flank fire for over one fourth of a mile. Having driven the enemy to the top of a hill at the far side of the field, my men came suddenly upon a heavy force of the enemy and was driven back to a fence, when I succeeded in rallying a portion of my men with others of the Brigade, but was unable to hold this position long. My orders were to be governed by the manuvers on the left, and having no support now on my left flank and being flanked then by the enemy, and being still exposed to the severe flank fire above mentioned, I ordered my men to fall back to a ridge to the rear where the Reg't was reformed. Everything was done by myself and [my] officers to keep the men at their post. I never saw the men fight with more spirit and gallantry in my life. The officers did their part nobly, and if properly supported and not suffered to be flanked, there would have been no falling back. I lost two (2) officers missing, one (1) man killed, and fourteen (14) wounded, and twenty-three (23) missing.

Very Respectfully,
Your obedient servant
W. H. A. Speer, Lt. Col.
Commanding

Headquarters 28th N.C.T.
28th August 1864

Capt. E. J. Hale, Jr.
A.A.Gen'l

Sir, I have the honor to submit most respectfully a brief report of the part borne by my Regiment in the action of the 25th inst with the enemy at Ream's Station. Our position in the Brigade was with the 7th N. C. Reg't on our left, the 37th

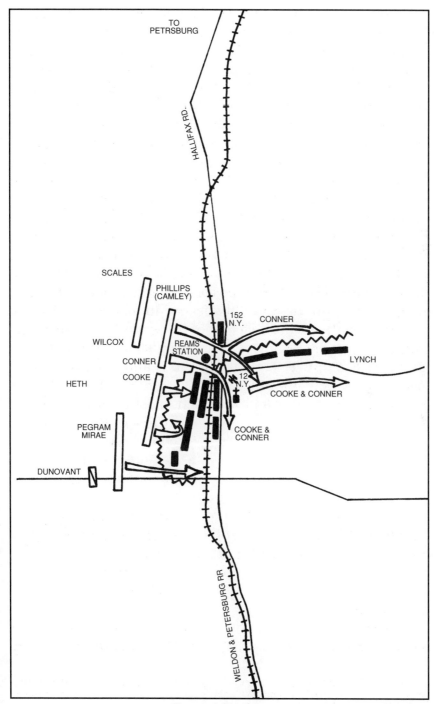

Reams' Station

N. C. Reg't on the right - governed by movements on the right. The Brigade was halted and formed on the right of the Ream's Station road for a while, then moved forward by the right flank circuitous one fourth of a mile — halted and moved to the left crossing the road to the station; halted as it were, after forming line of battle to support other troops, which soon became engaged with the enemy — after some time additional troops passed us forming on our right, we forming by moving somewhat to the left upon their line, were in due time moved forward with the entire line in a charge on the enemies works, which were found to be very formidable by us, not only regarding the difficult ground to pass over— of dense obstructions—but in approaching his works at an angle in which our Regiment was badly exposed and, for a short time, did fail to advance as rapidly as our friends on the right. But upon their better success, we were enabled to carry everything before us and did succeed in achieving what we believe to be the greatest victory of the war. The sacrifice was truly fearful in my Regiment. Col. Speer fell mortally wounded (doubtless). Capt. T. T. Smith of Co. B and five (5) enlisted men were killed instantly. Six (6) other gallant officers wounded—and twenty four (24) men, most of them badly.

> Most Respectfully your
> Obedient servant
> S. N. Stowe, Maj.
> Commanding 28th NCT

[Letter from Thomas G. Scott to William Harding of Yadkin County, N. C., August 27th, 1864, in private possession, cited courtesy of Frances Harding Casstevens.]

> Petersburg, Va.
> August 27th 1864

Dear Willie,

I sit myself to inform you of the late fighting. Your son Sammy[46] was killed the twenty-fifth of this month. I am sorry

---

[46]Asbury Speer and Samuel Speer Harding were both mortally wounded at the Battle of Reams' Station, south of Petersburg, Virginia. Their bodies were brought back to Yadkin County, North Carolina, for burial.

to inform you of the fighting. But I felt hit was my duty to write to you about Sergeant S. S. Harding. I am sorry to tell you of his death. He was shot through the hip. He did not live long after he was shot. I did not get to see him after he was killed. I was gone out with one of our men that was wounded and I did not get back till after dark. On the way, we was forced to fall back from the battlefield...I did not know that Sammy was killed till we was three miles from the battlefield. If I had of known that he was killed, I would [have] stayed there all night. But what I would of buried him, but I will tell you that I got all of his things. One of our company got through and give them to me. I have his knapsack and I have got his pocket book...I will tell you that Col. Speer was shot through the head. He will die if he all ready ain't dead now. I was sorry to loose my Col. and Sergeant. I will keep Sammy's things till you come after them if I can, for he was a good friend of mine.

T. G. Scott

[Letter from General Robert E. Lee to Governor Z. B. Vance, August 29, 1864. General Lee's letter, written the day Asbury died, complimented the North Carolina troops for their victory at Reams' Station. The letter was published in the <u>Wilmington Journal</u> in 1864 and reprinted in <u>Southern Historical Society Papers</u>, Vol. 9, (1881), pp. 245-246.]

Head-Quarters Army of Northern Virginia,
August 29th, 1864.

<u>His Excellency Z. B. Vance, Governor of North Carolina:</u>

I have been frequently called upon to mention the services of North Carolina soldiers in this army, but their gallantry and conduct were never more deserving the admiration than in the engagement at Reames's [sic] Station on the 25th instant.

The brigades of Generals Cook, McRae, and Lane, the last under the temporary command of General Conner, advanced through a thick abattis of felled trees under a heavy fire of musketry and artillery, and carried the enemy's works with a steady courage, that elicited the warm commendation of their corps and division commanders and the admiration of the army.

I am with great respect your obedient servant,

R. E. Lee, General

[Sheriff S. T. Speer to Governor Zeb Vance, Sept. 22, 1864, Vance Papers, North Carolina Division of Archives and History, Raleigh, North Carolina]

Yadkinville, N. C.
Sept. 22nd 1864

Dear Sir

It is made my official duty to inform you of the death of Col. Speer of this County, Senator elect from 44th district. He was wounded on the 26th [25th] ult. near Rheims [Reams'] Station on the back part of the head by a piece of shell, from the effects of which he died on the 27th [29th] ult. I wrote you some weeks ago, but as I have not read any order for another election, I presume it miscarried.

I have the honor to be

Your Obt. servt.

S. T. Speer, Shff.

of Yadkin

To His Excellency
Gov. Vance
Raleigh
N. C.
Sheriff S. T. Speer, Sept. 22, 1864

[Elizabeth Speer, W. H. A. Speer's mother, writes of her grief in this letter to A. Jackson Ashby. The original copy is in private possession of Helen Ashby Shull.]

August, 1867

Ever Dear Brother

I sit down to answer your kind letter which you wrote July the 27th. It gave me much satisfaction to hear that you was well and in the land of the living. I feared you was dead; it had been so long since I had got a letter from you. You don't know how glad I was. I can't express my joy and pleasure in reading from my only brother. As you know, Brother John died last July two years ago, as I wrote you in my last letter. Brother James, I know nothing about him. He talked of going to Florida when last heard from. I fear he is dead. I can't get any letter from Brother John's family; it has been a long time since I heard from them. There was two sons dead when last heard from. One died in the war and one son after the war closed.

In my last letter to you I told of my bereavement. My oldest Son Asbury was killed in the Rebel Army. He was Col. in the 28th North Carolina Regiment. He was killed at Reams' Station. My poor heart bleeds when I think of my poor child being murdered. It was no better than murder to make men go to the army and get killed. He lived four days after he was wounded; a piece of shell struck him in the head and broke his skull. He was in his sense all the time and said to those that stood by, he should soon be where there was no war, that he had given his body to his country and his soul to God. If that be true he is better off than to be here in this troublesome world. I have had seven children. They are all gone but two. One of them lives with us, the other a few hundred yards from us. He has two small little boys, four and two years old. The youngest married last spring a smart little wife.

We are doing as well as we can. We have plenty now but we shall be scarce I fear another season. Crop can't be half crops, let the season be as it will, there is hundreds that will not make bread and many will not make seed owing to the wet in the spring and the drought in the summer. There was not a good wheat crop. Some made a little while others made some to spare. Corn and wheat is very high [but] there is not much to sell. Some thinks corn will bring one dollar at the heap. Bacon is scarce, not much to sell. It will not be had at all next summer, I fear at no price. The hog cholera is raging in this country, as [a] great many have lost all they have got and they can't get any to fatten. There appears to be no cure for it. Poor people is bound to suffer. We could

Elizabeth Ashby Speer (1804-1890)
Like her husband, Aquilla, Asbury's mother, Elizabeth,
believed people in the South had "rebelled against [their]
maker and against [their] government and...could expect
nothing but judgment from the Almighty." She wrote, "I
wish I was away from this rebel state." Elizabeth Ashby
Speer was my great great great grandmother.

not expect any better. The nation is so sad. It is a wonder we are spared and have as much as we do. It is better than we deserve. We have rebelled against our Maker and against our Government, and we could not expect nothing but judgment from the Almighty. Our country is in great distraction. I feel awful when I think of the state of things in this country. I wish I was away from this rebel state. I never wanted to leave the old South until they seceded from the old United States. If I was not so old I would try my best to persuade the rest of the family to move. But it looks like folly to break up now. We are so old and settled and have everything around us to render us comfortable, for we can't have many years to spend. I am now in my 64th year and I shall soon be the way whence I shall not return. I don't feel like I could live many years, although I may live longer than I expect. I am able to do tolerable work, yet can walk two or three miles.

I would like to see you and your family and would be so glad if you could come and see us. I seem almost to see your face smiling at me like you used to do when I would come down to Father's. You would run and say yonder comes Betty and hold up your little arms for me to carry you to the house and then you would gabber and tell me something that had taken place since I was there before. You was very good and was counted pretty. You was so much like Mother, more so than any of the children. I am still trying to get to the Good World. May the Good Lord direct you and me and ours that we live so that when we come to die, in peace with God and all Mankind, [we] can say all is well. All is well from your devoted sister.

Elizabeth Speer

[Elizabeth Speer died in 1890 at the age of 86. She outlived all of her children except James.]

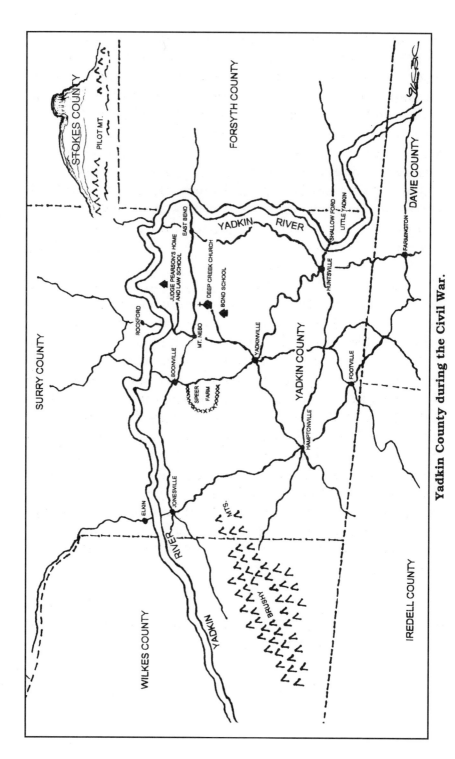

Yadkin County during the Civil War.

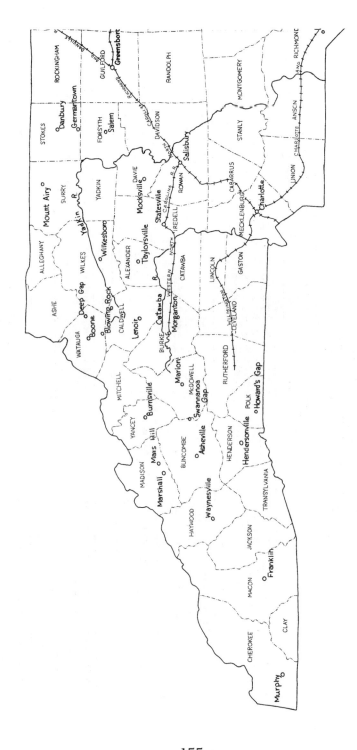

1861-1865 map of Western North Carolina, used by permission of the Department of Cultural Resources, N. C. Division of Archives and History

FAMILY TREE FIGURE 1.

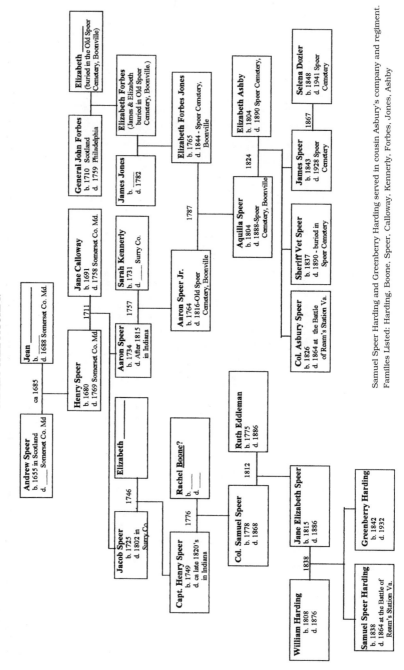

Samuel Speer Harding and Greenberry Harding served in cousin Asbury's company and regiment.
Families Listed: Harding, Boone, Speer, Calloway, Kennerly, Forbes, Jones, Ashby

FAMILY TREE FIGURE 2.

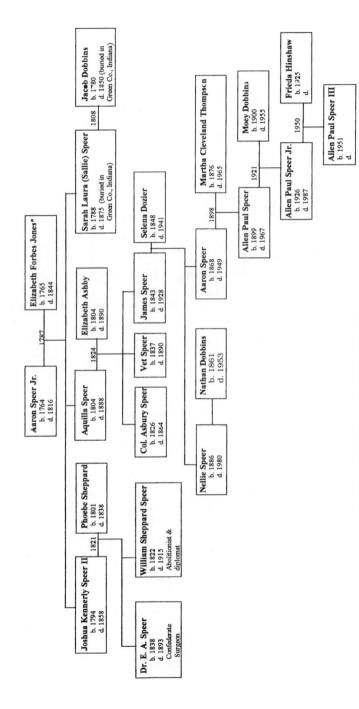

*granddaughter of General Forbes, b. 1710, d. 1759 in Philadelphia (see Family Tree Figure 1.)

Families listed: Speer, Sheppard, Dobbins, Dozier, Thompson, Hinshaw, Forbes

FAMILY TREE FIGURE 3.

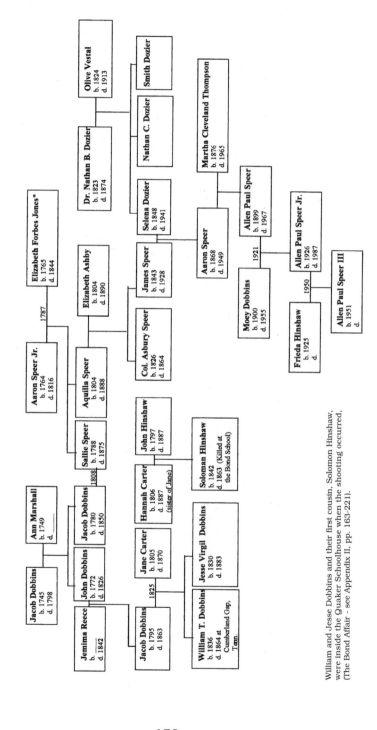

William and Jesse Dobbins and their first cousin, Solomon Hinshaw, were inside the Quaker Schoolhouse when the shooting occurred. (The Bond Affair - see Appendix II, pp. 163-221).

CHART SUMMARY
from Andrew Speer to Allen Paul Speer, III

Generations

1st	Andrew Speer, my seventh great grandfather, was born in Scotland and came to Somerset County, Maryland from County Donegal, Ireland.
2nd	Henry Speer, my sixth great grandfather, lived and died in Somerset County, Maryland. Another sixth great grandfather, General John Forbes, forced the French to abandon Fort Duquesne during the French and Indian War. Forbes renamed the fort, Fort Pitt, which later became the city of Pittsburgh.
3rd	Aaron Speer, Sr., my fifth great grandfather, moved to Surry County, North Carolina — now Yadkin — in 1771. Another fifth great grandfather, Captain James Jones, married Elizabeth Forbes, the daughter of General Forbes. Many of the Speers served under the command of General Forbes during the French and Indian War (1756-1763).
4th	Aaron Speer, Jr., my fourth great grandfather, was a farmer and teacher. Aaron's first cousin, Captain Henry Speer, fought in the American Revolution.
5th	Aquilla Speer, my third great grandfather, was the father of Colonel William Henry Asbury Speer. Aquilla's cousin, Colonel Samuel Speer, was the son of Revolutionary War soldier, Captain Henry Speer. Colonel Samuel Speer fought in the War of 1812.
6th	James Speer, my great great grandfather, was the brother of Colonel Asbury Speer. James did not want to fight for the Confederacy. The 6th and 7th generations of the family fought against each other. Some Speers were pro-Union, while others supported the Confederacy. Some Dobbins cousins served in Asbury's company and regiment, while others joined the Union army. Dozier, Harding, and Hinshaw cousins also served under Colonel Asbury's command in the 28th Regiment N. C. Troops.
7th	Aaron Speer, a nephew of Colonel Asbury, was my great grandfather. He married Martha Cleveland Thompson.
8th	Allen Paul Speer, my grandfather, married Moey Dobbins, a great great great granddaughter of Jacob Dobbins, the first Dobbins to settle in Surry County — now Yadkin County.
9th	Allen Paul Speer, Jr., my father, married Frieda Hinshaw, a cousin of Solomon Hinshaw, who was one of the conscripts killed at the Bond School in 1863. Many people of my father's generation did not know how many pro-Union families there were in Yadkin during the war, partially because painful and unpleasant topics were known to have split families, churches, and communities in the past.
10th	Allen Paul Speer, III. With the help provided me by cousins Lewis Shore Brumfield, Francis Harding Casstevens and J. D. Long, I was able to put together a family tree, and uncover some of the hidden secrets that caused so much mental and emotional anguish for my family during the Civil War.

APPENDIX I

PRECINCT RETURNS FROM
YADKIN COUNTY ELECTIONS

(1856-1861)

[From 1856 to 1861 Yadkin County was a bastion of Whig strength. After the war, most Whigs and some Democrats joined the Republican Party. Like other counties in western North Carolina with divided loyalties, Yadkin citizens blamed the war on the Democrats. For well over a hundred years, Republicans have refused to let Democrats control the politics of the county.]

1856 Election

	House of Commons		Governor	
	W. H. A. Speer (Whig)	Crawford W. Williams (Democrat)	John Gilmer (American Party)	Thomas Bragg (Democrat)
Mt. Nebo	47	139	49	130
Jonesville	155	50	148	62
East Bend	99	142	110	122
Huntsville	134	57	141	52
Hamptonville	293	81	297	88
Total	**628**	**369**	**745**	**354**

[Voting returns for Yadkinville precinct could not be located at N. C. State Archives. John Gilmer was a Whig leader in North Carolina. In this election, he ran as a member of the American Party. Thomas Bragg was the brother of General Braxton Bragg.]

1858 Election

	House of Commons		Governor	
	W.H.A. Speer (Whig)	Crawford W. Williams (Democrat)	Duncan McRae (Whig)	John Ellis (Democrat)
Mt. Nebo	45	166	43	163
Jonesville	145	48	129	65
East Bend	110	137	96	138
Huntsville	120	55	112	48
Hamptonville	293	107	246	109
Yadkinville	120	228	131	214
Total	**833**	**741**	**757**	**737**

1860 Election

	Senate		Governor	
	W.H.A. Speer (Whig)	Joseph Dobson (Democrat)	John Pool (Whig)	John Ellis (Democrat)
Mt. Nebo	62	149	54	153
Jonesville	120	67	113	76
East Bend	102	142	101	141
Huntsville	122	37	120	37
Hamptonville	319	64	323	55
Yadkinville	172	284	188	274
Total	**897**	**743**	**899**	**736**

1860
Presidential Election

	Bell (Constitutional Union)	Breckenridge (Southern Democrat)	Douglas (Northern Democrat)
Mt. Nebo	45	117	0
Jonesville	138	46	5
East Bend	94	87	0
Huntsville	38	75	3
Hamptonville	264	47	2
Yadkinville	163	173	12
Total	**742**	**545**	**22**

[Abraham Lincoln received no votes.]

1861 (May 13)
Election of Delegate to State Convention
which Met to Vote on Secession

	Armfield (Whig)	Wilson (Democrat)
Mt. Nebo	64	72
Jonesville	179	5
East Bend	142	11
Huntsville	149	20
Hamptonville	152	46
Yadkinville	120	134
Total	**806**	**288**

[All the precinct returns from Yadkin County elections were found at the N. C. State Archives in Raleigh.]

Appendix II

THE BOND AFFAIR

The shootout at the Quaker school is only mentioned once in the letters written by Colonel Speer, yet the Bond Affair had a profound effect on his family. The most obvious impact, as it was for most Yadkinians, was the maze of strained relationships that it created for Asbury and the people he loved.

Inside the Bond School on the day of the shooting were two of Asbury's first cousins, Jesse and William Dobbins.[1] Jesse Dobbins was thought by many to be the ring leader of the pro-Union contingent in Yadkin. According to a story told by one of Jesse's grandsons, a tale he heard for most of his seventy years, "the home guard had instructions to try to kill Jesse first, because if he were dead the others wouldn't have enough sense to get away."

To further complicate matters, Asbury's brothers, Vet and James, were charged with rounding up Jesse and William and the other Union sympathizers. James Speer, who managed to avoid the draft by securing a legal deferment in the Home Guard, was ordered to enforce a conscription law he detested, while Sheriff Speer attempted to maintain order in a county that became more volatile as the war progresesed. Consequently, as war weariness intensified and as large numbers of deserters returned home to join up with the bushwhackers hiding in the woods, the lives of Asbury's two brothers were increasingly at risk (see the Joyce letter to Major McLean on page 199).

In addition, Asbury's parents, who already had lost four children to consumption, now faced the very real possibility of losing their entire family. It was the cruelest form of irony that confronted Aquilla and Elizabeth Speer who, from the outset of hostilities, had adamantly opposed secession. They now watched their three remaining children risk their lives for a cause they vehemently condemned.

A sensitive and introspective man, Asbury suffered with

---

[1] According to the Speer Family Bible, Sarah Laura (Sallie) Speer married Jacob Dobbins on December 25, 1808, which would make her a great aunt of Jesse and William Dobbins. Sallie Speer Dobbins was the sister of Asbury's father Aquilla. The Jesse Dobbins Papers, in possesion of Captain J. D. Long, also point out the connection of the Speer-Dobbins families.

Asbury's cousin Jesse Virgil Dobbins (1830-1883)
Jesse and William Dobbins, along with their first cousin,
Solomon Hinshaw, were Union sympathizers. After the
shootout at the Quaker school, Jesse and William headed
north to join the Union army. (Photo used by permission
of J. D. Long, a great grandson of Jesse Dobbins.)

his friends and family. Because of his sentimental nature and his love of home, he was horrified to see what was happening to the land of his ancestors. By 1864, he came to believe that "some national sin is hanging over us," and being a religious man, felt the likely outcome of the conflict would reflect the will of a just and merciful God.

Even so, he did not betray the South, or the men who served under him, or the neighborhood boys he had recruited to serve in his company. As he said more than once in his letters, "I am perfectly resigned to my fate."

The Bond Affair, along with the many aftershocks in its wake, would traumatize Yadkin County for generations. The subject remained taboo, as descendants instinctively knew that a mere mention of the topic would set off sparks and cause hard feelings. When I asked Aunt Nellie Speer Dobbins about the Civil War, the only response I could get from her was, "There was nothing civil about it."

Over a hundred years would pass before three of my cousins, Lewis Shore Brumfield, Frances Harding Casstevens, and Captain J. D. Long, would begin to unravel the mystery of the shootout at the Bond School.

Lewis Shore Brumfield, who for forty-seven years has tenaciously pursued the truth in the Bond Affair, first read an account of the altercation when he was fourteen years old. The description he read was published in the historical novel, *House Divided*, written by Ben Ames Williams. Novelist Williams did not change the names to protect the innocent. His account of the fight reads as follows:

> "Here's a letter from Gov. Vance about the latest trouble in Yadkinville," [General Longstreet said] "not far from your old home is it?"
>
> "Not far, no sir," [said Travis Currain].
>
> "Col. Joyce sent 14 good men to round up some of the deserters and conscripts the other day. The rascals took shelter in the school house. They killed Mr. West, the Justice, and John Williams and drove off the Colonel's men and escaped. Oh, I believe some of them were killed and wounded, but the rest

got clean away. They headed for Tennessee. What have you to say for those old neighbors of yours, Major?"

Travis hesitated, "I've known there was feelings."

"Feelings! By God, sir, that's a nest of traitors; That whole section. The entire population is banded together to hide the fugitives. An enrolling officer takes his life in his own hands if he shows himself there. And if Colonel Joyce's prisoners are brought to trial Judge Pearson will hold the conscription act unconstitutional and turn them loose."[2]

Novelist Williams had some of his facts straight. John Williams and a Mr. West were killed, as Lewis learned from Clerk of Court Lon West, a grandson of "Mr. West." Brumfield also learned from Lon West the names of the men indicted for murder, and saw the warrant for their arrest signed by Sheriff S. T. Speer, Asbury's brother.

When Brumfield talked to his great uncle, Rossie Shore (great nephew of John Williams), Shore did not remember the circumstances of how his Uncle John died. Brumfield also talked to Rossie's wife, Annie Pearl Dobbins, a granddaughter of Jesse Virgil Dobbins, the man accused of killing her husband's uncle and James West. Annie Pearl had no idea her grandfather Dobbins was charged with the murders. She did, however, know about the shootout at the Quaker school. Annie Pearl remembered her grandmother Dobbins had told her of "going up to the schoolhouse after the shooting stopped and the militia left, and treating the wounded 'Bushwhackers,'[3] asking where her husband was, what happened to him."[4] (He had escaped and was making his way north to join the Union Army). "It was the hardest thing I ever had to undergo," wrote Jesse Dobbins, "traveling 500 miles in wintry weather, mostly at night."[5]

---

[2]Ben Ames Williams quoted by Lewis Shore Brumfield, Timothy Williams Folks (Yadkinville: by the author, 1990), pp 117-118.
[3]People who hid out in the woods were called "bushwhackers."
[4]Brumfield, p. 117.
[5]Kathryn Dobbins Huggins, "Jesse Virgil and Sara Catharine Mackie Dobbins," in Heritage of Yadkin County, ed. Frances Harding Casstevens (Winston-Salem, N. C.: Hunter Publishing Company, 1981), p. 349.

Captain James West was killed at the Bond School House on February 12, 1863. (Photo used with the permission of Gladys West Haynes, a granddaughter of Captain West.)

When Jesse Dobbins returned to Yadkin County in the summer of 1865, Sheriff Speer attempted to arrest his cousin for the murders of John Williams and James West. Dobbins was quick to respond. "He spurred his horse and did not stop until he reached the Union army headquarters at Salisbury, returning with a column of Union soldiers and a Colonel who in no uncertain terms informed county officials that the affair was closed."[6] No murder trial was ever held. On May 10, 1883, Jesse Virgil Dobbins died of a heart attack at his mill (on what is now Dobbins Mill Road) and was buried near the Bond School in the Deep Creek Quaker Cemetery.

Buried in the same graveyard is another casualty of the Bond Affair—Solomon Hinshaw, first cousin of Jesse Dobbins. "Sol" Hinshaw was inside the schoolhouse with Dobbins when the shooting started, but unlike Jesse Virgil, Hinshaw was unable to escape. On his grave marker is written: "SOL HINSHAW, AGE 25, KILLED FEB. 1863 IN A SCHOOL HOUSE BY CONFEDERATE HOME GUARD BECAUSE HE WAS A UNION SYMPATHIZER."

History sometimes allows strange bedfellows in the same family. Some of these strained relationships are listed as follows: Solomon Hinshaw is buried beside his parents at Deep Creek Friends Church. His parents, John and Hannah Hinshaw, are my great great great grandparents. Jesse Virgil Dobbins is a cousin to my grandmother, and was related by marriage to Colonel Speer's niece, Nellie Speer, who also married a Dobbins. There are Dobbins graves in the Speer Cemetery and Speer markers in Quaker churchyards. The Confederate son of Crawford Wade Williams is buried at Deep Creek Cemetery, while Colonel Speer's Quaker aunt was laid to rest near his own grave at Providence Methodist Church. Killed Confederate militiaman, John Williams, was also a distant cousin of mine. His brother, Francis Kerr Williams taught slave children to read before joining the Union army. He later deserted.

---

[6]Huggins, p. 349.

Allen Paul Speer beside the graves of his great great great grand-parents John and Hannah Carter Hinshaw. Hannah Carter and the mother of Jesse Dobbins were sisters. Photo by Mike Joslin.

Allen Paul Speer beside the graves of his great great great great grand-parents John and Jemima Reece Dobbins. Jesse Dobbins was a grand-son of John and Jemima Dobbins. Jesse, John, and Jemima are buried in the Quaker churchyard beside Deep Creek Friends Meeting House.

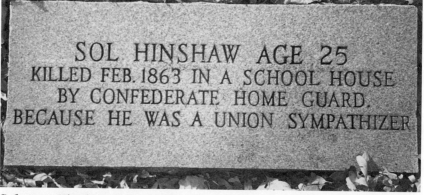

Solomon Hinshaw is buried beside his parents, John and Hannah, at Quaker Deep Creek Church. John and Hannah Carter Hinshaw are my great great great grandparents. (Photo by Janet Barton Speer.)

When Lewis Brumfield interviewed Jonah Williams, the grandson of John Williams, he learned why "Uncle John" was in the local militia instead of the Confederate army. According to Jonah Williams, his grandfather had eight little children to support.

The night Uncle John lay a corpse in his house on Shacktown Road, his youngest child, Lutie Peddycord, had just learned to walk, and she ran around the corpse half the night. Lutie Williams Peddycord was born March 6, 1862, so she was about eleven months old when her father was killed. She died in 1955, one day shy of her 93rd birthday.[7]

Of the four brothers of Brumfield's grandfather Ben Shore, "two deserted from the Confederate army. One went back and rejoined his regiment and was killed near Fredericksburg, Virginia. The other, Anderson Shore, was caught by the local militia and, along with his friend John Harville, executed on the spot near Anderson's father's mill at a place called Green Pond on the Huntsville-Courtney Road. The mill was burned and Harville and Shore were buried in the Harville cemetery."[8] It was random violence such as this that Yadkinians found reprehensible. Suffering with memories of

[7]Brumfield, p. 119.
[8]Brumfield, pp. 23, 48.

lost friends and relatives made social intercourse nearly impossible. A shroud of silence covered the county. The Civil War severed relationships, split churches and, for many, obstructed chances of reconciliation. Some people joined the Quaker church. Others became suspicious and withdrawn. William Williams Patterson,[9] Democratic candidate for sheriff before the war, was, along with Jesse Dobbins, Dr. Evan Benbow, and Wiley Shore, a founder of the Yadkin County Republican Party. However, the event that transformed Yadkin County was the shootout at the Bond School. Various accounts of the Bond Affair follow.

[Caleb Bond Hobson was the grandson of Reverend John Bond, who started the Quaker school. Colonel Hobson's letter to Dr. Nathan B. Dozier provides a context for the Bond Affair that occurred February 12, 1863, in Yadkin County, North Carolina. In 1956, Hobson's granddaughter, Minnie Speer Boone, wrote a biographical sketch of her grandfather that sheds light on her family's strained relationship during the Civil War. Many Yadkin families suffered the same fate. Hobson's biography is included below, and his letter to Dr. Dozier follows.]

Caleb Hobson [was] born in...Yadkin County, N. C., April 1, 1831. He attended the Friends Boarding School at New Garden, now Guilford College. At the age of twenty-five he went to his father with a story of his love for a girl who was not a Quaker. Marrying out of the Quaker Church was strictly forbidden. A father must disown a son or daughter who committed this offense or he in turn would be subject to a reprimand. His father argued and pleaded with him to no avail. Caleb loved his father and the Quaker Church too but he would not give up the girl of his choice. Sadly he returned to Duplin County where, on Aug. 10, 1856, he was married to Mary Eliza Oats without his father's blessing.

Shortly afterwards he took his young wife to visit

_____
[9]William Williams Patterson, my great great great grandfather, became a Quaker and strong Republican after the war.

The John Bond House
Reverend John Bond (1769-1860), a grandfather of Colonel Caleb
Bond Hobson, was an original member of the Deep Creek Monthly
Meeting of Friends (organized in the late 1700s). A founder of the
Bond School, Rev. Bond moved to Indiana only a short time before his
death. John Bond was my great great great great grandfather. From
the <u>Historical Architecture of Yadkin County, North Carolina</u>, Lewis
Shore Brumfield, editor. (Photo by Mike Joslin.)

The childhood home of Lieutenant Colonel Caleb Bond Hobson. (Photo
by Janet Barton Speer.)

his old home and the church of his boyhood. Stephen Hobson had been deeply disappointed in his son's marriage. No doubt the visit was a strain on all concerned. It was never repeated. But the breach might have healed in time, as Caleb did not live near them, had not other matters arisen which added fresh fuel to the flames. Mary [Oats] Hobson's father gave her some slaves as a portion of her marriage dowry. Holding slaves was a serious crime in the eyes of Quakers. Stephen Hobson was especially radical on the subject. He bought more than one slave just to set him free.

Then came rumors of war. Caleb, now living among Southerners, became fired with the zeal of Southern patriotism; he wanted to volunteer should the war become a reality. Here he ran afoul [of] another Quaker law. No Quaker was permitted to wear a uniform or bear arms in service. It is true that Caleb had been disowned by his father and his name stricken from the church roll but, to paraphrase Proverbs 22:6, "Bring up a child in the way he should go and when he is old it is not easy for him to depart from it." Caleb went to see his father and laid the matter before him. The stern old Quaker could only see that the disobedient marriage was leading his son farther and farther from the teachings of the church. Back in his own community Caleb was more convinced than ever that it was his sacred duty to answer his country's call. Before his plans were completed he made another long trip back to his old home to see if perchance his father might relent even a little. The unhappy interview lasted the long night through but the implacable father would not give an inch. Finally he announced this harsh ultimatum, "If thee persists in donning a uniform and entering the war then I never want to see thy face again." This was the last time any of them ever saw or heard from him directly. After he was killed his eldest brother,

William, wrote to the widow and sent her small gifts of money; another brother, Jesse, named his first son for him.

In 1862, C. B. (Caleb) Hobson raised a company of 100 men and went into the Confederate Army as Captain—later promoted to the rank of Lieut. Col. of the 51st Regiment of North Carolina. After the charge on Ft. Harrison, Va., Sept. 30, 1864, in which the Confederate Army was repulsed, he was reported "missing." (Ft. Harrison was located at Chaffin's Bluff on the James River.) Before any official message reached the family a comrade made a long ride to tell them that after the battle he had seen C. B. Hobson on the field—dead. In time the family received his camp chest containing his clothing; they never knew what became of his watch or his horse. The following is an excerpt from his obituary published in Duplin County, N. C. after the war:

"Had he lived to survive the battle he would have been colonel of the regiment. He was a brave generous hearted man. As he lived so he died doing his duty fearlessly. There was no man more brave than C. B. Hobson. He sleeps in Virginia, the sacred cemetery of the South. No marble slab marks his resting place, nothing to tell where he sleeps in peace. His family are in the 'Far West' (Pemiscot County, Mo.) without the fatherly care he so lavishly bestowed upon them. Duplin holds C. B. Hobson in grateful remembrance and is proud of him."[10]

[Letter from Lieutenant Colonel Caleb Bond Hobson to Dr. Nathan B. Dozier, Speer Family Papers.]

Camp Pender Dec 12 1863

Dr. N. B. Dozier

Your kind favor of the 17 last ult. come to hand a few days before we left Sullivan's Island near Charleston, S. C. and

---

[10]Minnie Speer Boone, Our Family Heritage (New York: The American Historical Company, 1956), pp. 36-38.

would have been answered but for the reason that I supposed we would be stationed at some point during the winter and, when settled, I would have a better chance to write you. But at present we have no assurance of going into winter quarters and may go from pillow [pillar] to post all the winter or in other words I am inclined to think that we will be kept in an active campaign during all this winter, consequently, I have no idea where we will be in ten days. I cannot even predict what developments one day of the future may make so I have concluded to write you a few lines, though I am in no mood to write at present, for I have been quite sick for some days____ though only a very severe cold settled on my lungs and in my back, though I think I will be well in a few days, provided I can keep from exposing myself too much. Your letter was quite a treat to me as I had not had a letter from any person in your section for a long time. You say you are glad I have so far succeeded in reflecting some honor on our connections in your section. I claim no honor for any thing I have done for I only feel as if I had done my duty, which I owe to my country, my family and my God.

My old Grandfather often told me that I was intended for some noble purpose, if I would only give my consent and my duty, and I think his words have now come to pass, for I am now embarked in the noble cause and have been for two years, I might say, and I think I will be blessed with health & strength to live through this war and see our independence declared. From what I have heard, I coincide with you in regard to the Bonds, Hobsons & Vestals[11] in your section, but Doctor, it does not become us to say so, for even an owl loves their young ones. Though with your consent I will make one or two remarks concerning them.

In the first place the young men are not responsible, for they have been tutored and trained from birth by the old cocks, and have more brains than mind. Their heads [parents], being full of ideas, taught them when they were babes.

---

[11]The Bonds and many of the Vestals were devout Quakers. Hobson's father, Stephen, was also devoted to the Quaker faith.

Consequently, they have no mind, judgment, or decision of their own. But hold fast to the old conclusion (I suppose) that a man must wear a certain coat and use the plain language even if it plunges him into torment. I cannot conceive that they are entirely ignorant of what is their duty to their country, future generations & their God. But I presume they say that they will do their duty to their God and every thing necessary will be added. But Doctor, as for my part, I would not give a farthing for a man's faith who would not pull off his coat or do any thing in his power to whip the Devil in order to save himself and household.

As for Religion, the Scriptures say a man who will not provide for himself & household is worse than an infidel. And a man who is not willing to shoulder his musket, if it is necessary, is not willing to provide for his family. So we may class the whole concern who act in that way or live as Tories.[12]

You may think that we have no such men in [the] Eastern part of the state. If so, you are very much mistaken, for there are hundreds of just such men as you speak of, only they are a thousand times worse than the Tories you name. Yes, we have men who own over 100 negroes who are Tories of so deep a dye that the Devil himself would not permit them to enter into his department. Yes, Doctor, when we look around and see hundreds of such men as these, who have hundreds of negroes to fight for stay at home by some kind ____ working scheme and act the Tory so full as they do, such men are Tories of what I call the double dye. There is not one man in a hundred who have firmness enough about him to say these men are Tories, for the simple reason that they are rich men. But, you know, I was always such a fool that I would speak my mind, let it affront or please who it may. When we see such men as these act the Tory so full, we must sorty [sort of] look over our poor connections for their acts.[13] But, Doctor, to tell you the truth, I have no use for any class of the Tories and I believe it would be a blessing if every Tory in

---

[12]Southerners still loyal to the Union were often referred to as Tories.

[13]Dr. Dozier married Olive Vestal, a cousin of Colonel Hobson. Many of her relatives were Quakers.

Olive Vestal Dozier (1824-1913)
Olive Vestal, wife of Dr. Nathan B. Dozier, is my great
great great grandmother. (Photo used by permission of
Frances Harding Casstevens, editor, <u>A Heritage of Yadkin County</u>.)

the Confederacy was hung in a line at one time between Heaven & Earth in view of our whole Army.

We left Charleston 29th Novm. and was one week coming to this place. We are now in camp here in Martin County 25 miles from Tarboro. We now have orders to hold ourselves in readiness to move, at a moment's notice, to Petersburg, Va. We stayed at Charleston for nearly five months, done lots of work and some good fighting. I think Charleston is safe. The Yankees have let time slip to take Charleston. You speak of high prices for provisions in your section. In my county, which is Duplin, the prices of every thing is much higher than with you, with only one exception, which is corn, and it sells now at the same price you name.

Congress seems to go to work like as if they were going to do something. It is thought by a great many that they will repeal the substitute act[14] and call upon all who have put substitutes in the Army to shoulder their musket and enter the service. I hope and trust they will. If so, it will increase our army considerable and not hurt many at home, for the majority of such men have done nothing to make money. I also hope that Congress will pass an act to place all the fine negroes in the Army who are able to bear arms. I am opposed to putting negroes in the Army, but Doctor, it seems to me that we will be compelled to do so in order to be able to meet the enemy we have to contend with. We will never consent to give a white man for a negro. Consequently, we must have negroes in our Army so we will be able [to] keep up the exchange of prisoners. My motto is for any & all means to prosecute this war until we gain our independence and drive those treacherous Yankees off of our land. We must not get impatient but press on. We must expect to see even worse privations than the present before this war closes. If not, we will be wonderfully blessed, more so than any nation in History. Well, Doc, I have filled up my paper and have not wrote any thing worth a cent, and will not interest you I know, but will do better next time. You will please let me hear from you.

---

[14]The Substitute Act allowed a person to pay a replacement to fight in his behalf.

Give my regards to Cousin Olly[15] and family. If you see Father say to him I am well & would like to hear from him. In haste, I remain yours truly,

C. B. Hobson

P. S. Direct your letter, Lt. Col. C. B. Hobson
51st R N. C. Troops
Petersburg, Va., Genl. Clingman's Brigade

[Letter from R. F. Armfield to Governor Vance[16]]
Dear Sir:

We have had a startling occurrence in this county of which you have doubtless heard before this time, which has greatly exasperated every intelligent and good citizen of the county. I mean the murder of two of our best citizens, magistrates of the county, by a band of deserters and fugitive conscripts.

The circumstances are these: There has been a strong feeling against the conscript law among the uninformed part of the citizens here ever since its passage. Many of that class swore that they would die at home before they would be forced off, and when the time came for them to go, perhaps nearly 100 in the county took to the woods, lying out day and night to avoid arrest; and although the militia officers exerted themselves with great zeal, yet these skulkers have always had many more active friends than they had and could always get timely information of every movement to arrest them and so avoid it.

The militia officers have been able to arrest very few of them. This state of affairs has encouraged the dissatisfied in the army from this county to desert and come home, until, emboldened by their numbers and the bad success of the militia officers in arresting them, they have armed themselves, procured ammunition, and openly defied the law. They have even sent menacing messages to the militia officers, threatening death to the most obnoxious of them and

---

[15]Hobson is referring to Olive Vestal Dozier.
[16]Robert Franklin Armfield (1829-1898) studied law with John A. Gilmer before opening a law practice in Yadkinville. Armfield later practiced law in Statesville, where he was elected to the U.S. Congress. Like his law teacher Gilmer, Armfield came from Guilford County Quaker stock.

Robert Franklin Armfield (1829-1898)
Armfield was the Whig delegate from Yadkin sent to the
May 13, 1861, state convention that met to vote on the
issue of secession. During the war, he was a Lt. Col. in the
38th Regiment N.C.T. and a superior court judge. After
the war, he was elected to the U. S. Congress. Armfield
was the first Master of the Yadkinville Masonic Lodge 162.

all who assist them.

Last Thursday 12 of the militia officers came on 16 of
these desperadoes in a school-house about 4 miles from this
town, armed, fortified, and ready for the fight. The firing
immediately commenced; which side fired first is not positively certain, but from the best information I can get I believe
it was those in the school-house. They finally fled, leaving 2
of their number dead and carrying off 2 wounded, after

killing 2 of the officers. In the school-house were found cartridges of the most deadly and murderous quality, made of home-made powder (one of the men known to have been among them has been engaged in making powder). Four of the conscripts who were in the fight have since come in and surrendered and are now in jail here, but the leaders and the most guilty of them are still at large; and the section of the country in which they lurk is so disloyal (I grieve to say it), and the people so readily conceal the murderers and convey intelligence to them, that it will be exceedingly difficult to find them, even if they do not draw together a larger force than they have yet had and again give battle to the sheriff and his posse.

But my principal object in writing this letter is to ask you what we shall do with those four murderers we have and the others if we get them? Suppose we try them for murder, do you not believe that our supreme court will decide the conscription act unconstitutional and thus leave these men justified in resisting its execution? I believe they will, and tremble to think of the consequences of such a blow upon the cause of our independence. It would demoralize our army in the field and bring first the horrors of civil war to our own doors and then perhaps subjugation to the enemy, which no honorable man ought to want to survive. I think I know Judge Pearson's opinion on the conscription act, and I believe that he is just itching to pronounce it unconstitutional. Suppose these men get out a writ of habeas corpus and have it returned before him and he released them (which he would be bound to do if he holds that they were only resisting the execution of an unconstitutional law with such force as was necessary to repel force from their person), do you not believe it would produce a mutiny in the army of the Rappahannock; and if it did not, how would you get another conscript to the field or keep those there who have already gone, or who could keep the loyal and indignant citizens at home from executing vengeance on these infamous murderers and traitors to the country?

These are considerations which alarm me, and I would like

to know what you think of them. Please write to me, and I will receive your opinion as confidentially as you may desire and ask. Could these men, and ought they if they could, be turned over to the Confederate courts to be tried for treason? Could the military authorities, and ought they to, deal with them? I hope you know I am conservative and for the rights of the citizens and the States, but for my country always, and for independence at all hazards.

Your obedient servant,

R. F. Armfield[17]

[Abram A. Willard was the son of Elkanah Willard, who was a brother of Benjamin, William, and Leander Willard, three of the conscripts present at the Bond School. Elkanah Willard was not at the schoolhouse when the fight took place, but he was with 33 people who broke into the Yadkin County jail and released three prisioners—William Willard, Harrison Allgood, and a man named Reed. (See Joyce letter to Major McLean, page 199, and J. M. Martin letter to Jesse Dobbins, page 207.) Tom Willard's condensed version of the original account of the Bond Schoolhouse fight, compiled and written by the late A. A. Willard, follows.]

The Bond Schoolhouse Fight

On the night of February 11, 1863, fifteen conscripts had met at the Bond Schoolhouse about one mile south of our home, their place of rendezvous to consult and lay plans to cross the Federal lines. Early next morning, February 12, 1863, a heart-rending scene occurred. During the night a light skiff of snow had fallen, and the sun arose wrapped in a mantle of snow. But a gentle breeze commenced blowing from the north early in the morning, rolling away the dark and gloomy clouds; and the sun shone out in all its beautiful splendor, casting a halo of peace and happiness on all around. The snow soon disappeared, but before the inmates of that house could

---

[17]O. R., Ser. I, Vol. 18, pp. 886-887.

give thanks to God and rejoice over the prospect of a beautiful spring-like day, a horrible scene transpired that chilled the blood in their veins and for a moment stopped the beating of their hearts. The news had been carried by some treacherous and disloyal person to James West, captain of the home guard, that the conscripts were congregated in the Bond School-house. He in the company with home guards and State soldiers hastened to the place, and while some of the conscripts were eating, and all listening to Jackson Douglas, who had just arrived with a news-paper, and was reading the news of the war, so eager were they to hear, they forgot to post a guard, and without a moment's warning, the report of a gun rang out long and loud upon the clear morning breeze and Solomon Hinshaw fell near the hearth with a bullet through his heart and died instantly, without a groan. At the same time a volley of shots was fired through the spaces between the logs, it being a log house, but none taking effect.

Immediately after Hinshaw fell, the Captain of the home guards appeared upon the door steps, and with an oath demanded the surrender of all within. One conscript answered, "I will surrender you d___ you," and leveled his gun, but just as he pulled the trigger, the Captain pushed the gun up, the contents almost cutting a joist in two over the door. Simultaneously, the report of another gun in the hands of another conscript rang out and the Captain sank upon the stone doorstep, a lifeless and headless form. The conscripts were panic-stricken and began to withdraw in disorder. Amidst the uproar and turmoil a voice cool and calm in the house was heard to say, "Boys, don't run, stay and fight to the finish." But that voice was not obeyed.

The first one to leave the house was shot and he fell mortally wounded with six bullets through his body. At the same time the conscript fell, another home guard was seen to place his hand over his heart, and was heard to exclaim, "Oh, my God, I am shot." He died in a few minutes.

The home guards, fearing recruits for the conscripts had arrived, also withdrew in haste leaving two of their number dead. After the firing had ceased, people from far and near hastened to the scene. Catherine Dobbins, knowing her husband was there, was the first one to appear upon the scene, the feelings of this noble hearted woman as she stood and looked upon the dead forms in the yard and the headless form upon the doorstep, can better be imagined than told. But her sad heart, even in the hour of great trouble was filled with joy when a wounded man who was growing weaker every moment from the loss of blood flowing from his wounds, told her that her husband had escaped unhurt. Jesse Dobbins and four other conscripts close together in their flight from the Schoolhouse battleground never stopped in their flight day or night until they crossed the Federal lines. After crossing over, they enlisted in the Union Army and fought for the Union cause until General Lee surrendered and the war closed.

On the day following the Schoolhouse battle, about 500 conscripts including my father and his three brothers left their homes, having for their leaders Alexander Johnson and James Reedy who had from time to time been successful in piloting many conscripts across the lines. Johnson and Reedy thought best they divide into two companies and different routes chosen, the Willard boys going with Reedy. Johnson was successful in taking his men through. But at Birch Mountain, North Carolina, Reedy was surprised and fired upon by the militia and home guards, killing many of his men. Some took to the woods and made their escape only to be captured, shot or left to starve.

Among the number taken captive were the Willard

boys. They were marched to Camp Vance,[18] but in a short time they made their escape from that camp. Warrants for their arrest charging them with murder were issued and the state militia was called for and was sent to assist in their arrest. They were recaptured in a few days after their escape from Camp Vance.

My father was left in jail at Morganton, Burke County, North Carolina, while his brothers were taken and placed in jail at Winston, Forsyth County, North Carolina.

The night after my father was placed in jail at Morganton he made his escape, after wading streams and suffering great tribulations and pangs of hunger, reached his home on the tenth day after his escape. When the report of my father's escape reached headquarters, it enraged the ones in command, and a detachment of State militia was ordered to march to Winston, take the Willard boys out of jail, and shoot or hang them. This detachment hastened to execute the order; they rode into Winston one morning before dawn and went straight to the jail arousing the jailer and showed him the orders and demanded of him to unlock the prison doors at once. When the heavy steel door swung open, the light from the candle carried by the jailer and those sent to execute them, revealed an empty room. They were stricken with wonder, consternation and amazement, but a hole in the wall, an improvised rope hanging down the outside wall were silent witnesses that the prisoners had once more escaped jail and unknown to them, their deaths. Bloodhounds were brought to the scene immediately; the dogs would stick noses to the rope, sniff the air, then positively refuse to take any trail. Shortly after this word of peace was heralded from the Atlantic to the Pacific Oceans, and Father and his

---

[18]Camp Vance was located in the Morganton area near Quaker Meadows.

brothers returned to their ruined and depleted homes, made so by vandals and the ravages of a bloody war, and to learn that a dark scourge of impending death imperiled their pursuit of freedom and happiness.

Jesse Dobbins, after receiving an honorable discharge from the Union Army, returned to his home. He rode to Yadkinville during court, while his friends were greeting him with a warm hand clasp, the High Sheriff stepped forward, grasped him by the arm and said, "Consider yourself under arrest." What is the charge against me? Dobbins asked. "Murder" said the sheriff. Dobbins' sudden movement of his person surprised the Sheriff and, freeing himself, he stepped back saying, "Sheriff, I have no ill feelings and bear no malice against you, and there has been enough men killed, but before I will submit to arrest under the charge of murder when I was fighting in self-defense, there will be more killed." So saying, he backed off and jumped astride a horse hitched nearby and rode in haste to Salisbury sixty miles away where a regiment of Union soldiers entrenched. Dobbins returned with them the next day. The soldiers surrounded the court house. Dobbins, the colonel, and three soldiers entered the clerk's office. There were several men present at the time. The colonel, after looking around, asked, "Which one of you gentlemen is the clerk of this court here?"

The clerk answered, "I am; what can I do for you?"

"What the hell is going on here?" the colonel asked. "Don't you know the war is over? You can get your damned old records and burn them." The clerk quickly gathered up the records and started to lay them on the fire. The colonel commanded him to stop and said, "It might be well for future reference not to burn the records. You cancel the charge of murder and all other charges if any against the conscripts." This command was promptly obeyed as the records show today.

After this, Father, his brothers and all conscripts came from their secret hiding places and set about rebuilding and replenishing their lost and ruined homes. During the days of Reconstruction, Father was elected to an office which he held for thirty-two consecutive years.

Here I will state as I do not wish to misrepresent any thing, that Father was not at the Schoolhouse on that memorable morning.

[The following account, published in the Yadkin Ripple, *February 14, 1906, relates other details of the shootout at the Bond School House; much of the information contained in this letter is also in the A. A. Willard account.]*

REMINISCENCES OF 43 YEARS AGO (Communicated.)

Editor, Ripple:

Just 43 years ago today, February 11, 1906, about sixteen conscripts had met at the Bond school house in Yadkin county, N. C., about one hundred yards south of where the Deep Creek Quaker meeting house now stands, their place of rendezvous, to consult and lay plans to cross the federal line. Among the number was James C. Wooten, Jesse Dobbins, William Dobbins, Horace Algood, Eck Algood, Robert Hutchens, Thomas Adams, Enoch Brown, Solomon Hinshaw, Jackson Douglas, Sandford Douglas, Anderson Douglas, William Willard, Hugh Sprinkle, Benjamin Willard and Leander D. Willard and if there was any others at that time, they are not remembered by the survivors of that memorable night and the vivid recollection of the heart rending scene that occurred next morning, February the 12th, 1863. During the night a skiff of snow had fallen, and the sun, on the morning of February the 12th, 1863, arose wrapped in a mantle of snow. But a gentle breeze commenced blowing from the north early in the morning, rolling away the dark and gloomy clouds, and the sun shone out in all of its beautiful splendor, casting a halo of peace and happiness on all around. The snow soon disappeared. But before the inmates of that house could give thanks to God, and rejoyce [sic] over the prospect of a beautiful springlike day, a horrible scene transpired that chilled the blood in their veins and for a moment stopped the beating of their hearts. The news was carried, by some treacherous and disloyal person, to James West, caption [sic] of the home guard, that the conscripts was congregated at the Deep Creek, or Bond school house. He in company with James Hanes, Henry Cowles, Jackson Shore, William Reynolds, John Williams, R. M. Gabard and about fifty others, hastened to the place, and while some of the conscripts were eating, and all listening attentively to Jackson Douglas, who had just arrived with a newspaper and was reading the news of war, so eager was they to hear, that they had forgotten to place out a guard, and without a moment's warning, the report of a gun rang out long and loud upon the clear morning breeze, and Solomon Hinshaw fell near the hearth with a bullet wound through his heart and died instantly without a groan, with a morsel of victual in his mouth, at the same time a volley of shots was fired through the spaces between the logs, it being a log house, but none taking effect except the shot that killed Hinshaw. Immediately James West appeared upon the door step, and with an oath demanded the surrender of all within, one conscript answered, I will surrender you d___ you, and leveled his gun, but just as he pulled the trigger, West pushed the gun up, the contents almost cutting a joist in two over the door. Simultaneously the report of another gun, in the hands of another conscript rang out and James West sank upon the stone door step a lifeless, and headless form, almost all of his head being shot off. The conscripts were panic stricken, and they began to withdraw in disorder. Eck Algood being the first one to leave the house, was shot, and fell mortally wounded with five or six bullet holes through his body, at the same time Algood fell, John Williams, another home guard, was seen to place his hand over his heart, and was heard to exclaim O! God, I am shot. He died in a few minutes. Amidst the uproar and turmoil, a voice, cool and calm, in the house was heard to say, "boys don't run, stay and fight to the finish." But that voice was not obeyed; they withdrew in disorder leaving two of their number dead and dying. The home guard fearing recruits to the conscript force also withdrew in haste and in disorder, leaving two of their number dead.

It has never been ascertained how many, if any, home guards were wounded in that battle. The wounded conscript was Enoch Brown, slightly wounded in left arm, Benjamin Willard wounded in left side and heel, Eck Algood, shot though the body. Before and after the firing had ceased at the school house, people from far and near hastened to the scene. Catherine Dobbins, who is now in very feeble health at her home, about two and a half miles north of Yadkinville, N. C. and widow of the late Jesse Dobbins, knowing her husband was there, hastened to, and was the first one to appear upon the scene, the feelings of that noble hearted woman, as she stood and looked upon that dead form in the yard, and that headless form upon the door step, and that form still in death within, and as she heard a voice weak and feeble, nearby calling to her, can better be imagined than told. But her sad heart even in the hour of great trouble, was filled with great joy, when Algood, the wounded man, who was growing weaker every moment, from the loss of blood flowing from his wounds, told her that her husband had escaped unhurt. Kind and sympathetic friends carried the wounded man to Lydia Bond's, who lived at that time, where our friend and neighbor, Aquilla E. Shore, now lives, where all earthly assistance possible was ministered unto him. But in great agony of pain he died the following day. Weeping friends carried the dead bodies to their respective homes, where they were prepared for burial.

This battle fanned the smoldering spirit of sectional strife into a flame, the conscripts was charged with murder. Warrants for their arrest was issued, the State Militia was called for, and was sent to assist in their capture. Jesse Dobbins, William Dobbins, Robert Hutchens and Thomas Adams, who remained near each other in their flight for freedom, started to, and in a short time succeeded in crossing the Federal line. They volunteered, but in about six months Robert Hutchens deserted, and in less than twelve months William Dobbins died while in service at Cumberland Gap, Tennessee. James C. Wooten, Jesse Dobbins and Thomas Adams remained and fought for the reunion cause until Lee's surrender and the South acknowledged itself whipped; they were given an honorable discharge and returned to their homes in Yadkin County, N. C. where Jesse Dobbins made himself a useful and respected citizen until his death many years after the war. James C. Wooten, a lifelong friend of the writer, is in very feeble health, and is now living in about one quarter of a mile of the Deep Creek battle ground. The last known residence of Robert Hutchens was New Castle, Indiana, Henry county. The whereabouts of Thomas Adams is unknown to the writer.

In a short time after the battle, Jackson Douglas was shot and wounded in one arm, by the home guard, the wound causing his arm to forever dangle, a useless member, by his side until his death, which occurred several years after the close of the war; through that disability he escaped the war. Sandford Douglas, Anderson Douglas and Hugh Sprinkle, facing a worse fate if caught, surrendered and volunteered. In a short time after joining the Southern army Sandford deserted, Anderson remained and fought for the Southern Confederacy until the end and the South subjugated. He was wounded at Ream[s'] Station thirteen miles from Petersburg, Virginia. The wound was of such a nature that it necessitated the amputation of his right arm near the shoulder. He and Sandford are both living near Yadkinville. Horace Algood was successful in keeping himself secreted until peace was restored. He is now living in a pleasant and happy home near Yadkinville. Hugh Sprinkle fought until the end and is now living near Yadkinville. Enoch Brown and the Willard boys made several unsuccessful attempts to cross the federal line. They in company with about five hundred others left Yadkin county, N. C., July the 10th, 1864, having for their leaders Alexander Johnson and James Reedy, who had from time to time been successful in piloting many conscripts across the line. Two brothers of our highly esteemed friends, the Editor of RIPPLE, was in that crowd, and neither of them ever lived to see their home again. As Johnson and Reedy thought best, they were divided into two companies and different routes chosen. Brown and the Willard boys going with Reedy, Johnson was successful in taking his men through. But at Rich Mountain, N. C. Reedy was surprised and fired upon by the Militia and home guard, killing many of his men, some took to the woods and made their escape. But only to be shot or captured. Among the number taken captives was Enoch Brown and the Willard boys, they were marched to Camp Vance, where they were held as prisoners, Brown and Willard boys as fugitives from justice. In a very short time Brown and the Willard boys escaped, but was captured time and again and held for a time in many of the various jails of Northwestern, N. C., but no jail could hold them long at [a] time. The last place they broke jail was Winston, N. C. A sister of the Willard boys secreted an auger and a chisel upon her person, left her home in Yadkin county and went to Winston and after undergoing a rigid examination by the jailor, she was permitted to go up stairs to see her brothers. When she left the jail she left the auger and chisel with them. With the auger and chisel, they bored and cut out of the jail and made good their escape, and avoided being shot or hanged, as a detachment of state militia had been ordered there to take them out and hang or shoot them, and arrived the day after they escaped.

Soon after this the welcome word "peace" was heralded from Florida to California, and from the Atlantic to the Pacific Ocean. And they like thousands of others, at the close of the war, returned to their shattered homes penniless. All indictments against them was nole prosceivied [sic]. Enoch Brown and William Willard have been dead for years, Benjamin Willard is now living out on R. F. D. route 3, Yadkinville. Leander D. Willard is living near New Castle, Indiana, Henry county, and is highly respected by all who know him. R. M. Garbard [Gabard], a personal friend of the writer, is living at Mt. Nebo Yadkin county, N. C. Henry Cowles, is and has been for years clerk of the federal court at Statesville, N. C., and so far as the writer knows he and Gabard are the only two home guards now living that took a part in the school house fight.

In proportion to the number engaged, that battle resulted in the greatest loss of life and the greatest number wounded of any battle fought during the late struggle between the north and the south. Eck Algood was buried in the Algood burying ground where the home for the unfortunate [county home] is now located in Yadkin county, N. C.

Solomon Hinshaw was buried at Deep Creek near where he was killed. John Williams was buried at the Williams burying ground near Spillman, N. C. James West was buried at Hamptonville, N. C. This narrative would not be complete without adding the following. On their way to the school house the home guard passed by the home of Daniel Vestal, about one mile away. West, the captain, in conversation with Vestal and his wife, who were old time Quakers, remarked that a number of conscripts were at the Bond school house and that he was going out there and take every D___ one of them prisoners. Mrs. Vestal answered "Yes, and thee will get thy head shot off thy shoulders too."

Whether or not the spirit of prophecy was upon Mrs. Vestal, we leave to the conjecture of the reader. But it is no less strange than true, it happened precisely as she foretold, and she always unto her death maintained the declaration that the horrible scene was revealed unto her before it occurred. The facts we write about occurred 41-43 years ago when a cruel war was raging and every mind and heart was filled with apprehension, and when men met their neighbors in deadly conflict. But now how changed the scene—peace, contentment and happiness reigns, and every mind and heart is at ease, and men meet with their neighbors to worship a just and holy Jehovah, and where once the sound of the gun was heard, and the battle field strown with the dead, shouts of new born souls can be heard as they catch a glimpse of the blessed gospel light, that will light the world forever more.

COL. HAM

Daniel Vestal House
Members of the Yadkin militia stopped here in February 1863 on the way to the Bond Schoolhouse. Captain James West of the militia said if he found any "bushwhackers" he would "blow their heads off." Mrs. Vestal, a strong Quaker pacifist who is said to have had presentiments, said, "Yes, and thee might get thine blown off, too." And indeed Captain West was shot in the head and killed. Until her death, Mrs. Vestal claimed the horrible scene was revealed to her before it occurred. (Photo by Mike Joslin. From the <u>Historical Architecture of Yadkin County, North Carolina</u>, Lewis Shore Brumfield, editor.)

Yadkinville July 30, 1864

Maj J. R. McLean
Camp Vance

Major:

My attention has been called by Mrs. Speer[19] to your letter of the 27th to her husband, the Sheriff. The Sheriff is absent and will be for a day or two and Mrs. Davis leaves here this morning for Camp Vance. I write to give you some information in regard to the "Yadkin refugees" now in your custody.

There are bills of indictment and capiases in the hands of the Sheriff against Wm, Lee and Ben Willard for the murder of James West & John Williams in the School House fight. Also against Enoch Brown and Hardee [Horace] Allgood who are said to have been captured with the Willards. These men are all conscripts and have been ordered into service and one of them, Allgood, is a deserter from the Army. It will not do to send them to the county to be imprisoned. Our jail is entirely unsafe, to say nothing of the danger of their being rescued by their friends as heretofore. Elkanah[20] did assist in forcing the jail a few weeks ago as can be proven. He did not try to disguise himself.

A very important question is, what is to be done with the balance of these men who went off in that company with the Willards. It is worse than idle to send them to the army, better turn them loose here, because if sent to the army they will be certain to desert and will bring arms with them and perhaps induce others to desert. Doubtless, some better meaning men were persuaded off with them, but very few. If these men are not allowed to get back to this county, we are now in a fair way to clean it out. At least the prospect is better than it ever has been. If

---

[19]Nancy Sheek Speer, wife of Sheriff S. T. (Vet) Speer, thought her husband's life was in danger.
[20]Elkanah Willard, age 33 in the 1860 Yadkin County census, lived in Mt. Nebo Township.

Nancy Sheek Speer (1839-1891)
Asbury's sister-in-law, wife of Sheriff "Vet" Speer, feared
for the safety of her husband after the shootout at the
Bond School. Nancy and Vet are buried at the Speer farm
on Cemetery Hill. (Photo by permission of Ann Speer
Riley.)

they come back we shall have terrible times. As to what should be done with the Willards, I can only suggest that they be kept in some very safe place until some action is taken in the matter.

Very Truly

[signed] W. A. Joyce[21]

I concur in the above. The Willards must not come back, and if they are sent to the army they will come.

[signed] Jos. Dobson[22]

I concur fully in this letter.

[signed] R. F. Armfield

Camp Vance
Aug 4th 1864

To Hon. R. W. Pearson
Chief Justice
Richmond Hill

In obedience to the fiat of the Writ to me directed in the matter of M. L. Cranfill,[23] I send herewith the body of the said Cranfill together with the cause of his arrest and detention. In the outset I desire as briefly as possible to recite, but somewhat in detail, the causes, remote and immediate, which led to the arrest.

It is a matter of "Common Fame," and I presume, well known to your Honor that, some few weeks ago, the public jail of Yadkin County was forcibly entered by a mob and the prisoners, three of whom, at least, were awaiting trial for murder, were released, and allowed to go at large;—that, shortly after this the town of Yadkinville was entered by a mob composed,

---

[21]William A. Joyce served as Deputy Clerk of Superior Court, Yadkin County. He was a Colonel in the Yadkin militia and, as such, was present at the shootout at Bond's Schoolhouse.

[22]Joseph Hughes Dobson, son of William Polk and Mary Hughes Dobson, ran against Asbury Speer in the 1860 North Carolina Senate race. Dobson's father was a first cousin of President James K. Polk, who as a youth visited the Dobsons at their home east of Rockford. The Dobsons were strong Jacksonian Democrats, going back to their connection with President Polk, a protege of Andrew Jackson. The town of Dobson in Surry County, North Carolina, is named in honor of the Dobson family.

[23]Martin L. Cranfill was listed as a physician by occupation, age 30, in the 1860 Yadkin County census.

The home, recently restored by the Yadkin County Historical Society, of Chief Justice Pearson. Richmond Pearson lived here for 30 years, where he conducted his law school. The Pearson home was about seven miles north of the Bond School. (Photo by Mike Joslin.)

it is believed, of the same persons who broke the jail, and, possibly, of the escaped prisoners,—and the arms and ammunition belonging to the Home Guard forcibly seized and carried off;—that immediately thereafter a crowd of these jail-breakers, escaped murderers, deserters from the army, recusant conscripts (some of them known to have been lying out for two or three years and desperately bad men,) escaped Yankee prisoners, and a few disloyal persons, over and under the military age, under the lead of one Alex. Johnson (charged with housebreaking and stealing in company with negro slaves in Davie County) about one hundred and fifty in number, left Yadkin County with the avowed purpose of going within the enemy's lines, and enlisting (some of them at all events) in the Federal Army.

Having been promptly informed of this movement, I dispatched troops to intercept them. About forty or fifty of them, including two of the escaped prisoners, the man who took the keys from the jailer, etc., were arrested in Watauga County near the Tennessee line, brought to this Camp and delivered to me.

On examination of L. L. Chamberlin,[24] A. A. Lindsay, Thos. Johnson & Wilburn Wright, who started to Tenn. with the party, & whom I send with this answer as witnesses for Your Honor to examine, I became satisfied that M. L. Cranfill knew that this exodus was in foot, knew the character of the persons engaged in it,—was guilty of aiding, assisting, and abetting deserters and recusant-conscripts in avoiding service in our army, and in going to the enemy,—and also, of assisting in the escape of felons charged with murder and other high crimes.

I, therefore, ordered his arrest for two reasons: 1st as a "military necessity", believing him to be a dangerous man, able and disposed to interfere with, and render negatory, efforts and plans on foot to arrest a band of deserters and recusant conscripts, known still to infest and disgrace the County of Yadkin.

2nd It was my purpose to turn him over, together with the witnesses to prove his guilt, whom I have under arrest, and all the information I had collected about him to the civil authorities for trial and punishment if guilty of Treason of any other crime.

To this end, before the Writ was served upon me, I had written Gen. V. Strong, C. S. Atty. giving information that I had such persons under arrest, and what I believed could be proven, and asking his advice as to what disposition should be made of them.

An early answer to this communication is expected.

I may add that another consideration has weight. I thought it probable that Dr. Cranfill as soon as he

---

[24]Lewis Chamberlin is listed in the 1860 Yadkin County census, age 27.

had an intimation that proceedings were about to begin against him, would do as he had advised others to do, namely, take French leave, and go to Tennessee.

I also invite your attention to enclosed copies of letters, written after it was known, by the writers, that orders for the arrest of Cranfill and others had been issued. They explain themselves: The one, signed by Shugarts, was written by Col. Armfield, Solicitor for the 6th Judicial Circuit, and was intended, I have no doubt, to embody his own views and convey them to me. It was the opinion of this distinguished lawyer, and sworn peace officer, that Adams should be arrested and detained.

Cranfill is just as guilty as Adams or more so, for he led and persuaded others, while Adams, being a man of much less intelligence, was probably induced by others to take a false step, of which he seems to have repented, as he, voluntarily, turned back. I was much gratified, that the course I had felt it my duty to pursue, met the approval of such eminent lawyers as Mr. Solicitor Armfield, and Mr. Dobson, and of so good a citizen as Col. Joyce, himself a judicial officer, and much more familiar with law than myself.

The other, by Col. W. A. Joyce ([Deputy] Clerk of the Superior Court), and endorsed by Mr. Solicitor Armfield and Mr. Dobson, shows the deplorable condition of things in the County of Yadkin, — the evident distrust, on the part of the most prominent and law-abiding citizens, of the power of the civil authorities to protect them in their person and property, and their strong desire for military inteference and arrests.

In conclusion, I may say that I cannot, without disobedience of orders, leave my post, and am indeed too unwell to do so, in order to appear before you in person, nor have I had time or opportunity to employ counsel. I have however written Solicitor Armfield and Mr. Dobson, presuming they will gladly appear for me, as they counselled the detention of Adams and others for offences similar to that of which Canfill [sic] is charged, and of which I honestly believe him to be guilty.

I enclose herewith notes of statements made by witnesses written down at the time of their examination before me.

All of which is respectfully submitted

J. R. McLean [signature]
Msj. Comdg.

P. S.

Since the above was written, I have had a conversation with Cranfill in which he admitted that he and his wife went to the spring in the evening that the crowd assembled there for the purpose of going off, before sundown, that Alex. Johnson and others were there - that he talked with him but declined to say what conversation passed between them.

He also admitted that he saw Johnson and others after dark, not at the spring, but declined to say what passed betwen them, how many, or who were in the crowd.

These admissions were made after he had been distinctly informed that he need not say anything to criminate himself, nor answer any questions unless he chose to do so.   J. R. M.[25]

[Letter from M. F. Farington to Jesse and William Dobbins, Westfield, Hamilton County, Indiana, in private possession, cited courtesy of Captain J. D. Long, grandson of Jesse Dobbins.]

August 28, 1864

Mr. Jesse Dobbins
Dear sir
     I take this opportunity of riteing [sic] you a few

---

[25]Richmond Mumford Pearson Papers, Manuscript Collection, Perkins Library, Duke University, Durham, North Carolina.

lines to let you no whare [sic] I am and how I am doing. I am well. I hope these few lines find you well. I am near Westfield Indianna [sic]. I am getting $1.25 per day for work. I left home the 11th of July last that was 136 of us Yadkin fellers started together but we got scattered and only 48 of us got here. Sandy Vestle [Vestal], John M. Martin, I. A. Warden & others, too tedious to mention, come out with us. R. S. Vestal and the Willard boys and several others got lost from us and I suppose were caught and taken back. I saw your wife the day I started for here and the children was well. Jane Sprinkle is still living with them. I think she will make enuff [sic] to do her. She has rented a part of the farm out and is tending a part herself. Me and Jackson Bovender threshed with your mashion [machine] last year and made your wife & mother 30 bushels of wheat a piece. Your father is dead. He died the Spring you left thar [sic]. He willed all his property to William Dobbins at his mother's death. All the property is thare [sic] yet. The Rebs [have] taken all of William's clothes and boots. I saw your mother the day I started. She is well and making anuff [sic] to do her. I have done all of your mother's halling [sic] since you all left. They have conscripted all from 17 to 50 and they are nearly all chased out and gon[e] to the army and out of here together. I want you to rite [sic] to me. This from

M. F. Farington

Get a furlow [sic], Jesse, and come out and see me and I will tell you all about things [in] N. C.

[Excerpts of a letter from J. M. Martin to Jesse and William Dobbins, October 2, 1864. Jesse Dobbins Papers, in private possession, cited courtesy of Captain J. D. Long, slightly edited for clarification. In this section of the letter J. M. Martin is answering some of Jesse's questions about the unstable situation in Yadkin County.]

New Providence Iowa

...as to who runs the conscripts I can hardly tell,
but they have a home guard composed of the
exempts and those that got off on account of disability. The worst there was in our settlement was John
Idle and some more of them town scamps and the
Boonville crowd. There has been some men killed
since you left—Ray Lakey, Solomon Green and
Alexander Brewbaker is all I recollect of at the present. They was killed by Capt. Snow's men.

Sizemore's boys is all at home. But Abraham, he is
in New Jersy. He was caught and taken to the army
and wounded and taken prisoner and took the oath.
I looked for him here this fall.

The rest got off on account of disability, but
James, and he has joined the Friends and that lets
him off. All the Willards started with us and Allgoods
but they did not get through with us. Douglass
Anderson [Anderson Douglas] is in the army with
Hugh Sprinkle. Jack was shot in the arm by the
guard and was at home in the bed when I left. Sanford was in the brush when I left. Noah Nisholas
[Nicholson/Nickols?], he joined the Friends and that
lct him off. Your unclc John Hinshaw's boys was all
in the army but Joseph. James was at home when I
left with one of his eyes shot out. Romulous Vestal
started with us and I have not seen nor heard from
him since we got scattered. N. H. Vestal and John
and Bond Vestal have all joined the Friends and that
lets them off. Your wife has some 4 or 5 letters from
you in the last twelve months and your mother got
one from William. I. A. Warden stopped in Hamilton
County, Indiana. His post office is Westfield. As to
[the] Wagoners, I cannot tell anything about them.

Your Father was sick some five or six weeks. They
had two doctors with him. They said it was the cancer he had on his ear that killed him. He did not complain of much misery, only such weakness and

burning in his breast and stomach. He grieved a good deal about you when he was first taken sick, but he became satisfied that you was out of the reach of the rebs and then he seemed to be glad that you was out of their reach. Aunt Anna Mackie died with newmony [pneumonia] but let their disease[s] trouble you no more than you can, for it is a debt we all have to pay sooner or later, and their change was a happy one. They both seemed willing to die if it was the Lord's will.

Rebecca Carter lives with your Mother and has ever since your father died.... William, I am sorry to hear of your affliction. I think it would be good for you to come out here, for this is a healthy place, and the wind blows very pure and sometimes rite [sic] smart cool too. Your father died last May, [it] was a year ago. Henry Stalling and Joshua Steelman have both joined the Friends and that lets them stay at home. It is so about the conscripts turning the prisoners out. They went there one night and demanded the keys and the jailer gave them up, if they would not hurt him. [He] opened the doors and let them out. They was 33 of them that went to let them out. There was only 3 in jail, that was William Willard and Harrison [Horace?] Allgood and [a] man by the name of Reed, who was accused of _____. They started with us but they was in the other company and I have not heard whether they have got through or not.... Well, William, the rebs have taken all of your good clothes and some chickens was all that they [had] taken from her [your mother]. Enoch Brown worked five months for your mother last summer and fall. He soon got well of his wound. The bullet is in his arm yet. He started with us but was in the other company and I do not [know] whether he has got through or not.

[Letter from Jesse Dobbins to Sarah C. Dobbins, cited courtesy of Captain J. D. Long. Slightly edited for clarification.]

Straw[berry] Plaines Tenn
June the 19 A. D. 1865

Most respected Companion,

I once more am Blest with the opportunity of writing to you to let you know that I [am] well at this time, truly hoping that when these lines come to hand, that they will find you and all of the inquiring Friends well. I was sorrow [sorry] to hear of Nathan and Jesse [Mackie] a being captured and sent off with the filthy rebs. But I am glad that it is no worse than it was. If they had a bin caught at home the tanyard would have bin burnt for furnishing leather to shoe the lawless scoundrels that has murdered so many of our union friends. I heard that there has bin a great many of our County boys murdered since I was driven off by the traitors.

It was the hardest thing that I ever had to under go when I had to start, to leave you and the dear little children in the enemy country and start a distance of 500 miles, knowing that we would have to travel in the night time. So we did and had to wade creeks and rivers, as we come to them many times after wading the waters, we was so near tired down and so sleepy that we would lay down in the woods and go to sleep and, when we was a bout to freeze, some of us would wake from our sleep and call to the rest to get up and start. Our clothing was froze some times so that we could hardly move our joints and we was some times three days and nights without any thing to eat. We was 4 weeks a giting through to whare we could go whare we pleased. We stopped at London Kentucky and rested. We had no money and we told the tavern keeper that we could not pay him and he told us that he did not want any pay. He kept us three days and nights and when we started to Lexington, whare we volunteered for the purpose of forcing the armed traitors out of our Country, or submit to the Laws of our Country.

The traitors did not have the pleasure of murdering my poor brother but I do believe that they was the cause of his death. The cold that he got when we was going out I think was the cause of his death.

The War is over now and I think that I will soon be at home with you and the children. And you and all of our people can say with truth that I never aided the rebellion of the theaving murderers. With all of the privations that I have had to undergo I am truly [thankful] to my God that it is as well with me as it is.

Robert E. Hutchens has acted badly.[26] I am truly sorrow [sorry] that he had done as he has. I talked to him about his conduct but it did no good. I went up to Greenville the other day and when I got off of the cars I saw some woman a getting out of the cars. And on looking around I saw that it was R. E.'s [Hutchens] wife. She was a crying. All of her children was dead but the youngest one. She had a stay at the hospital in Nashville Tenn and had not heard from R. E. since coming in to our lines, until she came to Knoxville the other day and saw James Wooten. He was in the hospital. He is mustered out.

Now we will be at home soon. We will all be at home as soon as we can be mustered out. If you have any chance send word to uncle Pleasant [Dobbins] that Miles tis well and doing well. He will be mustered out very soon and so will Cousin Levy Burcham. I want you to take care of your self and not work to[o] hard, because you are left to do all your self. I had rather you would hire your work done. I have got money enuff to live upon until I can make more. So ends hoping that our next communications will be in words in stead of letters.

[The following excerpts from the diary of Jesse Dobbins have been slightly edited for clarification.]

---

[26]Dobbins is referring to the fact that Hutchens deserted from the Union army.

Jesse Dobbins of Batry B, First Tenn, Light Artilery, enlisted at London, Ky. the 27 of February 1863 and was Discharged at Nashville Tenn on the 20 of July 1865.

A small sketch of items thru the War of 1861.

During the first year I thought that North Carolina had more good since [sense] than to follow South Carolina but to our great misfortune we Submited to what is called the gag laws until we was carryed off by a minority of Black h[e]arted office seekers. The[y] tolde us that they were union men up to the call for 75 thousand Troops to inforce the Laws of the United States and then I saw that they did not want the union. The[y] only intended to hide in the office by pretending to be Union, up to 1862, then Governor Vance rode in to the govenors office on the Conservative Horse knowing that he could not get in to office by running as a Disunion candidate.

There has never bin a day since the State aborted out of the union that it would not come back if they would stop the gag law and let the union cause be fully explained. I think that the Union men had the same cause to rebel against the so-called Confederacy as our fore fathers had to rebell against the british government. For we have suffered tackzation [taxation] without representation. The officers came up as wolves in sheeps clothing while all the screams was going on.

I thought that I would never be called to fight so much against my principles but I had a great many hard things to incounter with. I was called a Tory and every other hard name and my condition was such as I could not help my self. For I had a loving wife and two dear little helpless children that I could not leave as long as I could be any benefit to them.

In November of 1863 [1862] there was a detail made up in our County for the purpose of getting salt halde [hauled] for our County and I went on a trip to the Virginia salt works [Saltville, Virginia], for which I got very little pay for and when I returned with my salt I wanted enough to salt my pork at the same rate that others paid for it. But it was objected to by a man that happened to have more Black children than I had white ones. But notwithstanding all of that, I was willing to make another trip rather than to leave my family but they [Confederate officials] decided I would do them more good in the rebel army than I would a halling salt so they sent armed force after me without notifying me the first time, just as if i was some theaf [thief].

But I got the news before they got thar and made good my escape. This was January about the 20, 1863, and from then up to February the first I kept my self in priveat [private] places until the 2nd day of February. They came a snow that covered every place that I had selected for my safety and the conscripts became generaly alarmed, and began to get into badges [buildings?] for the purpose of defending them selves and myself and about fifteen others took [refuge] in a school house in my own District and took what fire arms we had with us to defend our selves with, provided that we was attacked. And we staid there unmolested until February the 5 1863. [Date is incorrect; should be February 12.]

In the evening about three o'clock P. M. we was attacked by a greater number of the enemy but we repulsed them until we made good our escape with this loss of two of our side killed and two wounded. The enemy loss was two killed and then we stayed two days in that county [Yadkin] and then started to Kentucky on the 7 of February 1863 [wrong date, February 14] and marched 4 days and reached Watauga County N. C. wherein was stopt by the Home Guard so called. Thar we had to tell a non Truth. We told them that we was a going to Abington Va. to join the reb Army and we stayed there 4 days and then we saw a Lieutenant that had a company at Big Creek Gap, Tenn near the Kentucky line and he gave us a pass and transportation from Warren Va to Knoxsville, Tenn on the Virginia and Tenn railroad and the pass that the Lieutenant gave us carryed us safe to the Cumberland mountain.

We left Knoxville for Big Creek Gap but when we reached Clinch Mountain, there we found a friend that had been a pilot for the Union men all the time since the war [began], and he took us to a house and had supper got for us in a short time and he went with us all that night and we had to wade one creek that night that was so deep that we had to strip off our clothing not knowing whether we could wade it or not. But we crossed without mutch difficulty and then we found friends plenty all the way thru to Kentucky. Then we found Union men plenty on the 28 day of February. We landed safe in London Ky where we staid for days and rested and then started to Lexington.

We marched 75 miles to Nicholasville. There we took the train and went to Lexington, Kentucky and stayed there three weeks and then volunteered for the 4th Ohio battery, where we remained two weeks and then was transferred to the first Tenn battery where we have remained until February the 2, 1864. Up to this [time] we have not bin in any regular engagement. Our batery has bin in three skirmishes but has not had one man hurt yet in battle or from sickness.

It was a hard trial for me to give up [and] to stay away from my family but I could not do any better for them nor myself for if I had a stayed there I could not labor in my cornfields nor go to [my] mill for fear of being caught by the rebs. Besides that my family was always uneasy. So I could not earn my board. Thus I was willing to join the United States army for the purpose of fighting for the Libertys of my Dear country that is more precious than gold. There is not but [only] two sides to this question. One is to tear down the best form of government that ever ruled a nation. And the other party is fighting to preserve that government and to drive despotism from the face of our free and happy Country. The rebs say what are you coming down South for? We answer them correctly, "to release our friends that you have been guarding with the bayonet for three long years." The rebs say that I am a traitor to my country. Why? Tis this because I am for a majority a ruling and for keeping the power in the people....

I will state something about my private affairs. My life has been a lonesome one ever since I was driven from my family, but the last twelve months has been more trying to me. My only Brother [William] was taken sick the 8th of June, 1863, and has been very weakly ever since, until the first of October, 1864 [when] he was taken with something like the fever and lived until the 16th of November. At half past 9 o'clock, he quietly departed this life. I stayed with him from the time he was taken down as long as he lived, and then I had him put away. Hope I did all that I could for him. But he's gone to a better world than this. [On] the 23rd day of October, he said that he was going where there was no more war nor Rebels.

After having been driven from my loving wife and dear little children and had not heard anything from them in the eighteen months, on the 21st of September, I had the pleasure of reading a letter from under the hand of my Dear Companion which brought me the sorrowful news of the death of my father...

[On] the 2nd of July, our company was mustered out and we started for home on the 15th and reached home on the 7th of August [1865].[27]

[Diary of William Dobbins]

---

[27]The diary of Jesse Dobbins is in possession of a descendant, Captain J. D. Long, Greensboro, N. C., and reprinted here by permission.

W. T. Dobbins

In the commencement of this war I was a union
man and I told the rebels that I did not want a Confederacy and I would not fight for it. And I passed on
then until the Conscript law was passed and then
they thought they had me then, but I guess they
missed. They sent after the rebel guard, unbe-
knownst to conscripts, and they came and before I
knowed that they was in the county, they was standing all around my bed with their guns, a ordering me
to get up and go with [them] to town. And seeing that
I was overpowered, I had to surrender to them. And
they took me out and tied me like a thef or a mur-
derer because I would not fight for the Confedercy.

And I would not! I hate it! And they drove me
around all night until about daylight. And then they
put me in jail and kept me there one day and night
and until two o'clock the next day. And [then] the
jailer opened the door to let some ladies out that had
went in to see their husbands. And as the[y] went
down the stairs, I went behind them and the jealer
[jailer] didn't see me until I got [within] reach of the
door. And he said "hold on there," but it was of no
use. For I rushed right over him and made my escape
and they never ketched me any more.

Then they threatened to kill me on first sight. And
then I armed myself and layed out in the woods. And
in that time we was fired on one night and we
returned the fire. But no damage was [done on] ether
side. And we passed on til the 5th of Febarury [12th
is the accurate date]. And the rebels attacted us
again in the Quaker School meeting house, and we
had a pretty smart fight. There was two killed on
each side and some wounded but they never ketched
nary one [of us] alive.

And the night of the 5th we tramped about 8 miles
and we stayed there all day that day. And the next
day we started for Kentucky; that day was Febarury

— 215 —

the 7th [14th] 1863. We traveled that day and all night. The next day we took to the woods and traveled the most of the time in the woods for three days. And then we came out and traveled the roads. We traveled the roads one day and stayed that night at Mr. Brown's. And starting [out] next morning, we traveled til about eleven o'clock that day. And we was halted by the rebel home guard at the Cold Mountain.

[William's account of events stops without explanation at this point. His next diary entry is in May 1864.]
[My] health is very bad yet Brother is well. We are in Cumberland Gap, Tennesse.

May the 29 1864. W. T. D.
I am in the hospital.

June the 12, 1864
We are yet at the Gap. I am in camp. I am not well. It is very cloudy and raining this morning.

W. T. D. June the 19, 1864
[We are at] Camp in Cumberland Gap Tennesse. We are at the Gap now and I am not well. Jesse is sick and in the hospital.

July 4
We are at Cumberland Gap and they are a giving salutes today.

July the 6 1864
Camp at Cumberland Gap, Tennessee.

August 6, 1864
We are at Cumberland.

August 14, 1864

W. T. Dobbins
Born in 1836, 28 years old. I am in the hospital at
Cumberland Gap, Tennessee.

October 23, 1864
At the Cumberland Gap. I thank God that I can say
that I do believe that the good Lord has pardoned my
sins. William T. Dobbins[28]

[28216]Diary of William T. Dobbins, brother of Jesse Dobbins, who died in 1864. Copy in possession of J. D. Long, Greensboro, N. C., and used here with his permission.

Index